8 GREAT FLIX

JOHN HOLWAY

Copyright © 2019 by John Holway.

ISBN: Softcover   978-1-950580-56-9

All rights reserved. No part of this book may be reproduced or transmitted in any form or by any means, electronic or mechanical, including photocopying, recording, or by any information storage and retrieval system without express written permission from the author, except in the case of brief quotations embodied in critical reviews and certain other non-commercial uses permitted by copyright law.

Printed in the United States of America.

To order additional copies of this book, contact:
Bookwhip
1-855-339-3589
https://www.bookwhip.com

CONTENTS

Monet's Daughters 1

Bessie Coleman's Flying Circus 8

A Valley in Spain: Steve Nelson 32

Ace of Diamonds: Bert Shepard 48

Margaret and Joe: MC Smith 78

Captain Combat: Charlie Bussey 85

The Witch in the End Zone (Zap the Pats) 112

Solveg's Song (Love Among the Peaks) 154

MONET'S DAUGHTERS

DASHING YOUNG YANKEE ARTISTS DESCEND ON THE MASTER'S HOME IN GIVERNY, AND THE QUIET FRENCH VILLAGE WILL NEVER BE THE SAME.

ESPECIALLY THE GIRLS.

"PARADISE IS FOUND," ONE YANKEX CLAIMS,
"AND WAITS ONLY TO BE ENJOYED."
UNTIL THE OLD MAN FINDS OUT. THEN THERE
IS HELL TO PAY.

In 1887 a rickety train puffs through a quaint Norman village. Artists Theodore Robinson, Wilfred Metcalf, and John Leslie Breck spy three girls gliding in their boat. The guys lean out the window and wave and call. Then they exchange glances, nod vigorously, and when the train squeals to a stop at the next station, hastily gather their bags and painting easels, and pile out.

The inn-keeper, Mme Baudy, takes one look and slams the door. They hastily wash at the village pump and knock again. This time she admits them.

She also mentions that Claude Monet himself lives in town.
Huh?!

Next day they timidly knock at the great man's door, and he invites them to lunch to meet his family, including his step-daughters - the girls in the boat! They listen entranced to Metcalf's broken-French tales of living with the Zuni Indians.

That summer, while Monet is off, painting cathedrals in Rouen, the guys and gals dally hand-in-hand among the hills. The asthmatic Robinson pairs off with a local girl, known only as Marie (above).

Monet and Breck agree to paint together. Breck arrives with easel and palette outside the master's home. "*Un Moment*," Monet smiles, and soon Blanche appears, pushing a wheelbarrow with two easels and paint boxes. She nods to Breck to put his in, which he does, then takes one handle, and they head for a field of haystacks.

"So you're an artist too?" John says .

"And, very good," Monet nods. "She's had her own exhibition in Paris." Blanche drops her eyes modestly, but lets a coquettish smile lift the corners of her lips.

They set up easels. Nearly finished, Monet steps back, cocks his head, quickly mixes some blue and red, and dabs at the canvas. Breck and Blanche steal a glance and do the same.

As the afternoon light casts new shadows, they fold their paint boxes. Monet walks over to inspect their work. "*Pas mal*," he nods - "not bad."

(by Breck)

(by Robinson)

(by Mecalf)

Winter. Monet departs to the south of France to paint the sunny Mediterranean. Back home, couples swirl on skates and steal kisses beneath swaying Japanese lanterns under the moon.

More Yanks arrive, plus British writer Robert Louis Stephenson, and the inn is soon jumping on Saturday nights. The boys unlimber guitars, and, marvels one Frenchman: "I thought I had stumbled into *le* middle-*ouest*. Bearded men, huge *athletiques* dressed like lumberjacks, drinking, shouting, smoking, arguing" while "*un grand diable* banged lustily on the piano."

Next day they sober up while Mme Baudy enjoys a well-earned cognac.

Then Monet returns and finds out what has been going on. Breck is ordered home. But a new threat arrives - another American artist, Theodore Butler, sweeps Suzanne, Monet's favorite model, off her feet.

Monet storms. "He will *not* have his daughter marry an artist! And an *American* artist, at that!"

But at last he softens, dons a top hat, and leads Suzanne from the village church, a scene that Robinson immortalizes.

When Marie names Robinson the father of her child, he is also ordered home. He will die of ashthma in New York.

Breck becomes a strong advocate for Monet and popularizes his work in America. He dies at age 39, possibly a suicide.

Suzanne dies early, Butler marries her sister, Marthe, and Monet happily dandles his grandkids on his knee. In 1914 the family sails to safety in America.

Blanche marries Monet's son, Jean. She may have assisted Monet on his final masterpiece, the Water Lilies panels, and cares for him until his death in 1924.

In 1944 an elderly Blanche hears a knock on the. German General **Erwin Rommel** asks if he may visit the home. She nods but says, "I won't shake hands."

"I understand," he says.

- 0 -

The Pugeot bumps along the dirt track to a river bank beside a crumbling *chateau*. A small rock cairn bears a fading sign:

Ici en 1944 nos allies,
les gallants Americains,
ont fait le premier
croisant de la Seine

BRAVE BESSIE'S FLYING CIRCUS

THIS PRETTY HALF-CHEROKEE, HALF-BLACK DAREDEVIL FLIES LOOP-DE-LOOPS, DAZZLES MEN, AND PUNCHES HOLES IN THE SKY FOR BLACKS TO FLY THROUGH.

"I'M SURE A MOVIE OF YOU, PROPERLY ACTED, WITH PLENTY OF ACTION, WOULD BE A BIG HIT."

R.E. NORMAN, PRESIDENT,
NORMAN STUDIOS, 1927

A SHERIFF AND SEVERAL POLICEMEN WALK AROUND THE WRECKAGE OF A BI-PLANE. NEARBY A POSTER ON A TELEPHONE POLE CARRIES THE PICTURE OF A PRETTY AVIATRIX

BESSIE COLEMAN'S FLYING CIRCUS

See America's only colored pilot
do a triple loop,
dance the Charleston on the wing, and do
THE LEAP OF DEATH
Sat, May 1 1927 Fairground
25 cents adults, 10 cents children

A rescue team pulls the mangled body of a man from under the plane. "He the pilot?" the sheriff asks.

"Yeah," a deputy says. He jerks a thumb. "The other one's over there. What's left of her." Near some houses beyond the field another crew searches the ground.

The sheriff pokes at the cloth fabric over the frame. His fingers easily go through it. A broken wooden strut sticks out of the twisted wing like a bone. He feels it with one hand and he is snaps it in two. Shaking his head, he continues his inspection.

"He's wearing a chute," he notes as the body is put on a stretcher. "Why didn't he use it?" "I don"t know. Maybe he didn't have time. Maybe he was too low."

"Who is he?"

"I don't know yet, but I think he's from Texas."

"And her?" He nods toward the ambulance.

"That little gal from Chicago, who does all that wing walkin' and stunt flyin'. Betsy or Bessie something. You know, the one that don't like separate white and colored seats."

"Excuse me," John Behncke, a young white man, says. "That's Bessie Coleman."

"Oh? Who are you?"

"I'm John Behncke. This is my plane."

"What do you know about this?"

"It looked like the pilot just turned upside down suddenly and dumped her out. Then he straightened up okay. If he hadn't hit that tree, he'd have been all right."

The sheriff arches his brow. "You think it was murder?"

Behncke shrugs.

The sheriff reaches into the engine compartment, tugs at something, and pulls it free. It's a monkey wrench. "I'll be daggone." They all look at it. "Now how did that get in there?" He pokes around some more.

"Coulda just slipped in from the pilot's compartment," the deputy says. "Don't look like nothing but some cardboard separating 'em."

"Maybe." The sheriff feels around. "Or somebody could have put it there. Now who would want to kill a little colored gal" She have any enemies?"

"Don't know," the deputy says. "But you know how people talk."

The sheriff looks at him hard. "What do you mean?"

"Well, you know, like coloreds shouldn't be doin" this stuff." The sheriff thinks it over and waits for more. "A lot of colored folks was against her too, didn't think gals should be foolin' around with stuff like this.... And then, you know, a lot of guys were chasin' her." The sheriff listens. "Some white guys too - you know how it is."

A cabin in east Texas. Three little girls sprawl on the floor in front of a fireplace. The eldest, Bessie, 13, is reading *Uncle Tom's Cabin* aloud. The two younger ones listen wide-eyed. But Bessie slams the cover shut. "No sir! I ain't't gonna be no Topsie. I'm gonna join the Wild West Show and ride the buffaloes."

"They don't have girls in the Wild West Show," says Georgia, 10.

"Do *so*! Annie Oakley's in the Wild West Show. She can shoot better'n any man."

"Yeah, but she's a white gal."

"Well, I'll be an Indian gal - the Indian Annie Oakley. I'll be Princess Flying Cloud. I'll hang from a trapeze like they do in the circus, and I'll do a flip in the air and shoot a cigarette out of my lover's mouth before I hit the ground. And Daddy will come back from the Indian reservation and give me a big hug, and...."

"Will not. You'll be too scared."

"Will so. Won't I, Momma?"

Momma, a large black woman, rocks and listens. "Yes, honey, and you'll marry your lover and have a lot of babies just like me and your daddy did, and you'll make a lot of nice clothes for 'em."

"Will he go away like Daddy did?" Bessie goes over for a hug. Momma kisses her eyes. "No, dear, he won't have to. He won't be an Indian, and you won't be in Texas. The only thing worse than bein' colored in Texas is bein' an Indian in Texas. But Daddy loved you, honey, and he didn't want to leave his baby." The others want their affection too. "All his babies," Momma adds with a kiss for each of them.

A cotton field at noon. Bessie, 17, seem taller than 5'3". She wears a long skirt and apron and drags a bag hanging from her shoulder as she moves along a row. She takes the full bag to be weighed and to get her pay. Then on the way home she stops at the back door of a white home to pick up a basket of laundry for Momma to do.

"Shoot, this ain't no life," she mutters, wiping her brow with a forearm. "I'm gonna chuck all this and go to Chicago with Walter and be a dancer."

At the Waxahatchie station, Bessie in her Sunday best stands in long line at the "Colored Tickets" bus window with her worldly goods in a cloth satchel in one hand. There is no line at the white window. In her eyes we read the fear of leaving home and the excitement of going off to the big city. She gives Momma a brave hug and bends to smile reassuringly at Georgia.

She alights in the Chicago station. White folks carry their suitcases and hail cabs. Blacks, like Bessie, look bewildered at their first sight of the City. She clutches a piece of paper with her brother's address. On the street, she asks a passer-by, "Sir, my brother is Walter Coleman, he's a porter on the railroad, he lives at 65th Street and Wentworth." He points her toward the South Side, and she begins walking, gradually leaving the white world behind and going deeper into the black world.

Comiskey Park. Lines of fans file into the park while across the street, wearing a black and white uniform and cap and with a finger

wave in her hair, Bessie is sitting in the window of a barber shop, manicuring nails. She has a twinkle in her eye and gives her customer a coquettish pat on the forearm as he gets up to leave.

His seat is taken by **Jesse Binga,** a black gangster, lottery king, and wheeler-dealer, with spats, rings, and a long cigar. Binga has already done time as a racketeer and now owns the biggest black bank in America. He extends his hands to her with a wink, then turns to hold court with his sycophants about the odds on today's game. He leaves Bessie with a flashing smile and a a ten-dollar tip.

At night Binga and Bessie stroll through the crowded sidewalks of the black nightclub district with another couple - teen-aged singer **Josephine Baker** and dancer **Bill "Bojangles" Robinson.**

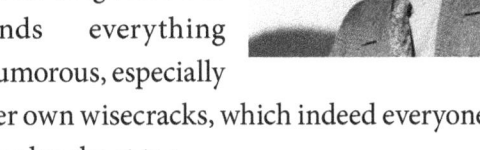

Baker is still an unknown, but she wears a big smile and finds everything humorous, especially her own wisecracks, which indeed everyone else laughs at too.

Robinson, already a star, does some fast fancy stepping to avoid another couple and beams as the others clap.

They turn into a smoky club, where **King Oliver'**s jazz band, with

Louis Armstrong on cornet, is playing "Muskat Ramble."

A dapper politician, **Oscar DePriest,** stops at their table for an introduction. "How are you, Alderman"" Jesse greets him grandly, introducing the party.

"Don't let that grand jury give you no hard time! They're just jealous because they don't want to see a colored man go to Congress." DePriest asks Bessie to dance, and she takes the floor in a bright red dress with rows of fringe. The other couples

move away to let her have the center of the floor. Armstrong, taking his inspiration from her, blows even stronger into his cornet.

At the barbershop an elegant man in his 40s sits down at her table. **Robert Abbott,** editor of the Negro Chicago *Defender*, asks her to dinner.

At a nice Chinese restaurant he tells her she shouldn't be seen with a gangster like Binga. She's got more in her than that, and he wants to see her develop it. Negro women have so much to offer the race, he says. His own aunts had established churches in Atlanta. Excited, she responds by pouring out her dreams of being somebody.

But she can't stay away from Binga either. From his chauffeured auto she watches with him while his guards with sawed off shotguns transfer sacks of money from an armored car to his bank.

Walter goes to France with the Army. Photos and headlines of flying aces fill the newspapers.

In the race riot of 1919, gangs of whites roam the streets with torches, shouting, "Come out and get your asses whipped, or stay in and get 'em barbecued." Bessie, Momma, and Georgia bar the doors and huddle together.

SCENES FROM FIRE IN IMMIGRANT NEIGHBORHOOD "BACK OF THE YARDS"

The *Defender* headline screams:
38 DEAD, 500 HURT

Walter comes back from France with tales of Notre Dame and champagne and the French girls - they even fly airplanes. Slightly tipsy, he taunts her: "You can't do that."

"That"s it!" she explodes. "You just called it for me."

She applies to a succession of white flying schools, and at each one the instructor shakes his head no.

"Go to France!" Abbott says. If she'll go to school and learn French, his paper will sponsor her trip. It will be good for circulation. Bessie throws her arms around his neck.

She tells Binga. But she can't afford to quit her job to study. He has a solution: He has foreclosed on a chili parlor and has some cash. He unrolls a wad of bills and peels off three hundreds. She stares at them. "And bring me back some nice Paris dresses," he says, peeling off two more bills. Bessie embraces him for a long kiss. "Heh," he says at last, "you'll burn the chili!"

Bessie's ocean liner dock in Le Havre with multi-colored streamers, blasts of the horn, waving people on shipboard and at dockside.

At a French airfield she meets the dashing wartime ace, **Charles Nungesser**, and in halting French asks to enroll with him. He listens with great attention. But as they talk, a woman  student cartwheels her plane into the ground with a big explosion. They sprint to the wreckage. At last he tells Bessie, "I am sorry, *Mademoiselle*, but, as you see, for the women it is *trop dangereux*."

However, a pretty girl is hard for a Frenchman to turn down, and after dinner with wine in a quiet cafe near the Seine, Bessie enrolls.

She wakes before dawn and dresses - shiny boots, puttees, a Sam Browne officers" belt across her chest. She adds a leather coat with fur collar and tops it off with a soft-billed cap, which she fits at various angles until satisfied.

Then she leaves her Paris apartment as the early morning

tradesmen are making their deliveries of bread etc, and trudges through the suburbs and into the countryside to the her first class.

At the air field the *petite Americaine* in the stunning uniform, turns the heads of the otherwise all-male students, and Nungesser has trouble holding everyone's attention as the gather beside a plane, a World War I Nieuport, made of cloth and wood and held together with wire. It has no brakes, uses a tail skid for a third wheel, and reaches a top speed of 80 miles an hour.

Nungesser offers to give her special help after class with the French aviation phrases she will need, to the great disappointment of her classmates, who had been jockeying for the honor of driving her back to Paris.

In a shimmering pink dress of sequins and fringe, Bessie takes his arm in a smoky nightclub off the Champs Elysees, packed with "Apache" dancers with slicked hair, open shirts, and tight skirts.

Then they join the crowds on the Champs who flock to a more fashionable club. On the dance floor, Bessie does a mean Charleston with Nungesser and returns to the table perspiring.

The manager, **Eugene Jacques Bullard**, comes to the table. He is black, with the broad shoulders and rolling gait of a boxer and the military bearing of an ex-soldier and fighter pilot in the French air force. Nungesser leaps up to embrace him as an old comrade. "Permit me to present *Mademoiselle* Coleman," he says.

"*Enchante, Mademoiselle,*" Bullard says, kissing her hand formally, then snapping his fingers to summon champagne.

"This is Jacques Bullard, my old and dear friend," Nungesser continues.

Bullard asks permission to ask Bessie to dance.

"Where y'all from, Miz Coleman?" Gene asks, switching to a Georgia dialect. This surprises her.

"From Texas, Mister Bullard," Bessie says. "I used to chop cotton. And you sound like, let's see, Alabama?"

"You"re close," he smiles. "Georgia. I'm half-Indian, can you tell?"

She does a double take. "Yeah?" - switching to Chicago argot - "Me too! Cherokee."

"Creek. And what brings you to Paris?"

"I've come to learn to fly and drink champagne," she laughs. "I'm going to be the world's first Negro pilot."

"Oh?" he teases. "You seem to have mastered the second. But do you think colored people can fly airplanes?"

Her eyes blaze.

"Well, I'm sure they can," he says quickly. "But you're a *woman*!" (Teasing her:) "Everyone knows a gal can't handle a plane. It's too big for her and complicated. Also too dangerous. She'd panic in an emergency."

She sputters in angry speechlessness.

"Besides, you should be home in the kitchen cooking and raising babies."

She beats on his chest with her fists.

"OK, OK. Just kidding, just kidding! If you can fly like you can punch, you'll be a great pilot."

He spins her around the floor, then guides her back to her table. "Thank you, *Mademoiselle* Coleman. I know you will be a wonderful pilot. And I wish you *bonne chance*, or as we say in Georgia" - he winks - "Y'all take ca-ah, Ma'am."

"Who is he?" Bessie asks Nungesser later.

"One of my dearest friends from the war. He shot down a *Boche* plane and received ninety-six bullet holes in his own ship."

Bessie is taken aback. "I never heard of him."

"*En Amerique, non,*" Nungesser shrugs. "But *en France*, we all love him."

Back at the airfield, Bessie takes the controls for the first time, and laughs with joy as she banks the plane and practices climbing and other maneuvers.

On her first solo, she bounces a few times on the landing and almost hits a wing on the ground, but she climbs out to the applause of the others, who shower her with much kissing on the hand and cheek.

Her arrival home in New York is attended by news reporters and photographers, as well as Binga and Abbott, each carrying a huge bouquet and trying to jockey the other aside. Bessie is wearing her most dashing flying uniform, an all-white one she had designed herself. She strikes poses while flashbulbs pop. Porters wheel three large wardrobe trunks down the runway after her.

The New York *Times* reporter asks about her instructor. "Oh, a *charming* boy. So gay. He shot down thirty-one German planes, you know. We just <u>loved</u> to fly high - the higher the better. You have never <u>lived</u> until you have flown." Binga and Abbott stir uneasily. Her age? "Twenty-three," she says blithely. Her admirers look surprised: She is really twenty-nine.

And her future plans? "I am having a *Nieuport de Chasse* [fighter] built for me, and I shall conduct exhibition flights in it. Our race must have aviators if we are to keep up with the times. I shall never be satisfied until we have men of the Race who can fly."

On the dock Binga grandly opens the sedan door and climbs in behind her, only to find that Abbott has already entered from the other side.

Squashed between them, Bessie is whisked

away to Broadway to see the colored revue, "Shuffling Along." She enters with a *beau* on each arm, and the audience rises to applaud - whites in the orchestra, blacks in the balcony. Afterward she goes backstage to meet the stars, **Ethel Waters** and pianist **Eubie Blake.**

In Chicago a reporter for the white *Herald* offers to do a story, suggesting that Bessie agree to pass as white. She shows up at the interview with Momma, who is obviously very dark. The interviewer stammers an excuse and backs out as Bessie tosses her head and laughs.

But Bessie is soon bored. "Now I have my wings," she tells Abbott. "What do I do now?" There are only a handful of women pilots in the United States, and most of them have to do parachute jumping or wing-walking in the flying circuses to make any money. "Look at Phoebe Fairgrave. She just made a jump of fifteen thousand feet. What do I do, jump sixteen thousand? They won't let women fly the airmail. And there aren't any woman barnstorming pilots."

"Good," he says, "then you'll be first."

"Nobody here will teach me."

"Then go back to France."

Back in Paris Bessie accompanies Nungesser to the *Follies Bergere*, where her old friends **Josephine Baker** and Louis Armstrong are advertised on posters out front. The lights dim, and the curtain goes up, revealing a jungle setting as a writhing Baker, clad only in a skirt of bananas, descends in a cage to sultry music. The audience applauds enthusiastically as she dances with several muscular males in loin cloths. After the show, Baker comes to their table for a joyous reunion of happy howls and hugs.

A Chicago movie house advertises "Bessie Coleman in France." Binga and his entourage go in. Flickering newsreels show Bessie with Nungesser beside a plane, then shots of their plane flying upside over Paris. Binga stalks out.

Le Havre. Beside a waiting ship, Bessie and Nungesser watch arm in arm as porters carry her bags up the gangplank of a waiting ship. He kisses a tear away from her cheek. "I'll be with you soon," he says.

"I still wish you wouldn't try it," she says. "No one's ever flown across the Atlantic alone and …"

He hushes her with another kiss.

A blast from the ship's horn breaks the spell. she pulls away and slowly mounts the gangplank.

Back in New York Bessie holds another dock-side press conference. "Yes," she reveals, "I began flying during the War. I was a Red Cross girl in France, and I persuaded the French Air Corps to give me lessons."

"And how old were you then?"

"Eighteen," she replies, deducting two more years from her age.

Once again she goes from airport to airport, trying to enter air shows but is turned down. At Chicago's Checkerboard airport, Behncke, who is younger than she is, jumps nimbly from his plane,

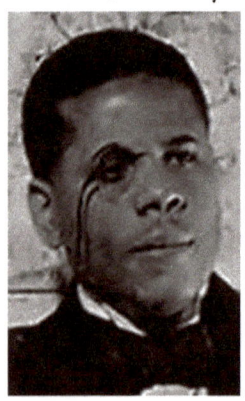

pushes his goggles back, and grins with hands on hips as he listens to her pitch. He owns the field. Sure, she can fly in his show. He even offers to lend her a plane. She spends more and more time at the field with him.

Bessie also shakes hands with strutting, monocled **"Colonel" Hubert Fauntleroy Julian,** the so-called "Black Eagle of Harlem." Julian, a six-footer beside the tiny Coleman, has a flair for self-promotion that approaches Bessie's own. He speaks with a haughty Jamaican accent and boasts of his flying lessons under the Canadian war-time ace, Billy Bishop.

Bessie has a brain storm. She'll fly and Georgia will do the "leap of death" from the wing. "No one has ever attempted this leap and lived," the *Defender* reports.

Bessie outlines the idea to Georgia, showing her the costume she'll wear. "It's easy," she says. "The parachute has a rip cord with a ring on the end. All you have to do is hold the ring and pull...."

"I will <u>not</u> do any such thing!" Georgia shouts.

"Oh yes, you will!" big sister Bessie replies.

"Have <u>you</u> ever made a "leap of death?'"

"Well, no, not yet, but...."

"But, hell! <u>I'll</u> fly the plane, <u>you</u> do the leap!"

Bessie calls up Julian. He not only agrees to jump from her plane, but he will play "Swanee River" on a saxophone on the way down.

Behind a military band marches tiny "Queen Bess, Daredevil Aviatrix," in a new red and blue uniform. Beside her the angular Julian marches with his sax. Both know how to play the crowd; Bessie blows kisses, and Julian makes sweeping bows as the spectators respond with cheers.

To the rousing strains of "The Star-Spangled Banner," Bessie guns the engine and lifts off. Julian climbs gingerly out on the wing, tries to stand, flails his arms wildly, and crouches down again. The spectators gasp. Bessie waves anxiously from her cockpit: "Go on! Go on!" Julian slowly stands, teeters on one leg, and the saxophone goes hurtling away as the spectators cry in horror. He hugs the wing struts, edging back to the plane's door. His foot slips, he hits the wing with his rump, loses his grip, and tumbles head over heals into space.

He wildly clutches for his ripcord. The hangar and little planes on the field below are quickly growing bigger as Julian plummets closer and closer. Bessie puts her hand to her mouth and gasps. Cries of terror come from the bleachers. Death seems inevitable. Then, miraculously, the chute opens. Julian struggles to find his shroud lines as he oscillates like a human pendulum out of control. A skylight on a roof rushes up to meet the Eagle.

Inside, three cops sit with their feet up on the desk when, with a great shattering of glass, Julian crashes down on top of them. While the crowd rushes to the precinct office entrance, the Black Eagle rolls over several times, getting tangled in his shroud lines. He scrambles up, hops, and falls. He struggles to get his harness off and at last stands erect.

Hearing the crowd outside, Julian adjusts his monocle and stumbles out, supported by the cops. He bows and waves to his public, then holds the cops' hands triumphantly in the air for the cameramen before turning grandly to accompany the officers, each on one of his arms, into his cell.

Meanwhile Bessie lands. The crowd runs to buy tickets for a five-minute flight.

The more flights she makes, the longer the lines get. Women especially flock to try it, sometimes dragging boyfriends along. "Ain't this great?" Coleman laughs to Behncke. "I bet more Negroes went up for an airplane ride today than in the whole history of the world until now!"

Binga has a proposal. He knows "businessmen" who are looking for a pilot to carry Chicago's finest Prohibition exports [bathtub booze]to thirsty clients in nearby states. "Uh-uh," she replies.

"Then how'd you like to be in movies?"

"Sure!"

"Well, this here is Mr R.E. Norman, the president of Norman Studios."

Bessie gives his hand a vigorous shake. "I'm the most famous colored person, man or woman, in the world, except maybe the jazz singers," she informs him.

"I'm sure a movie of you, properly acted, with plenty of action, would be a big hit."

"Not just on the HOBA circuit?" she asks.

Norman looks puzzled. "Hoba?" he asks.

"Yeah, you know - 'Hard On Black Asses' - those little movie houses in the Negro neighborhoods."

He laughs. "No, this will be seen by both white folks and black folks," he assures her. "Miss Coleman, you can pull the people into any theater."

Bessie grabs a pen and signs.

She arrives for the first day of shooting, wearing her latest flying togs, a stunning white with white boots and scarf. Norman meets her in the usual uniform - argyle sweater, knickers, and megaphone - and explains that it's the story of an ignorant bare-foot Texas girl with her clothes in a bundle on a stick, coming to the big city to seek her fortune. He shows her the tattered dress she'll wear in the opening scene. Bessie objects. "No Uncle Tom stuff for me," she sniffs.

When he insists, she sticks her nose up, turns on her heel, and stomps off.

"Black bitch!" Norman yells after her. "You'll never get another show in any state fair in America."

At her home, Binga throws up his hands in disgust. "I don't like all this flyin' stuff and movie stuff and runnin' around with white boys," he shouts at her. "Flying's not for girls. Kids and cookin', that's what you're supposed to do!" He stomps out, slamming the door.

Georgia passes him on her way in. "What was *that* about?"

"Well, that's it," Bessie sobs. "My career is over. No movies, no fairs, no shows, no plane, no money.... No man."

"What you gonna do now?"

"There's nothing else I can do," Bessie cries. "Open a flying school."

"How you gonna do that?" Georgia asks.

"I don't know," Bessie wails.

At breakfast Georgia is perusing the newspaper. "Oh, my God!" she gasps.

"What IS it?"

Slowly Georgia pushes the paper toward her with the headline:

NUNGESSER LOST AT SEA

Behncke gets her a job dropping advertising leaflets in California. At a Los Angeles airfield, she bumps shoulders with a pretty white flier with a tousled haircut.

"Who's that?" the flier asks idly.

"That's Bessie Coleman."

"Who's that?" Bessie wonders.

"**Amelia Earhart.**"

"I think she's called Amelia Earhart."

With the last of her money, Coleman buys an Army surplus plane, the Jenny. She'll unveil it at an air show in Los Angeles. Taking off to reach the field, her engine stalls on takeoff, the plane suddenly noses into the ground, and Bessie is pulled unconscious from the wreckage.

"Tell them to patch me up," she begs Behncke as soon as she comes to. "I have to get to Los Angeles in time for the show."

He kisses her forehead. "You know, you've got a broken leg and three broken ribs," he says.

Her brand new plane is also totaled.

Three months later Bessie hobbles out of the hospital, still in a leg cast. "As soon as I can walk, I'm gonna fly!" she declares. And she'll still open a school, where "our boys can master the air."

Momma throws up her hands. "I had thirteen children," she says, "raised up nine, and one of them was crazy."

Bessie recuperates in Mama's home, entertaining her sister's children with her impressions of blacks, whites, and Asians that keeps them howling with laughter.

But she's bored. Time drags on for two years. The papers have forgotten about her. Even Abbott has lost interest.

Bessie does have one caller, the **Prince of Dahomey** in French West Africa. She hurries to her closet to pick out her favorite Paris gown, only to find it missing. "Georgia! Where's that red gown with all the beads?"

Georgia admits she borrowed it.

"<u>Borrowed</u> it? Get it back here this minute!"

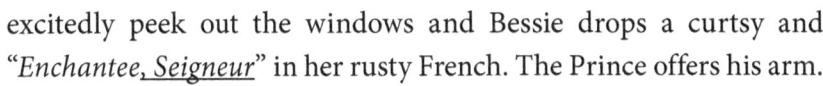

At last the Prince arrives as the little girls excitedly peek out the windows and Bessie drops a curtsy and "*Enchantee, Seigneur*" in her rusty French. The Prince offers his arm.

At last, a break. Behncke has found her a show in Houston, and she rushes there, telling the press, "My great ambition is to turn Uncle Tom's Cabin into a hangar for a flying school." She also confides that she is now twenty four years old.

The show will be on "Juneteenth," the day Texas blacks celebrate their emancipation. Bessie has an all-star cast. Iona McCartney, a white woman, leaps from one plane's wing to another's in mid-air. "Daredevil" Erwin, a white man, hangs by his teeth from a strap.

Bessie does barrel rolls, loop-the-loops, and figure eights. She climbs high into the air, then does a screaming dive almost straight into the crowd.

One white youngster tugs his father's hand. "I want to be a flier, Daddy," he says.

"Well," the father looks down, "I guess if a colored gal can do it, everybody can." On the ground Bessie looks for Liza Dilworth, who is advertised to be the world's first colored woman parachutist. But Liza has disappeared. So Bessie finds Behncke. "You fly," she says, hopping into the front seat. "I'll jump."

In the air, Bessie climbs out of the cockpit. The chute is in a canvas laundry bag tied to a strut. She hooks the chute's static line to her harness, tugs it apprehensively to make sure it's locked, crouches, and leaps, She lands in the center of the crowd, which erupts with an ovation.

After the show, Texas' colorful female governor, **Miriam "Ma" Ferguon**, gives Bessie a hearty slap on the back. "You showed 'em, gal," Ma laughs.

They are soon clinking glasses at dinner at the governor's mansion.

Christmas at Chicago. Bessie is stringing lights on the tree in her mother's house, surrounded by sisters, brothers, nephews, and nieces. Everyone is laughing. Her mother begs her to stop flying as too dangerous. The others all murmur agreement. Bessie tosses her head. "I gotta do it, Momma. I got these plans in my head. If I just do a little bit of what I want to do, everything will be all right."

She waves a farewell to them in the snow. Momma tries not to cry. Bessie smiles and gives her a big hug.

Bessie moves to Florida and lectures to crowded churches about the importance of Negroes not being left behind in the skies. She even invades a pool hall to bring the message to the men lounging there.

Bessie is also born again and accepts baptism.

And she meets playboy Edwin Beeman, the millionaire scion of a chewing gum fortune. He lives in his father's palatial estate, Beeman Park, and manages the ritzy San Juan Hotel. He is also married. Eager to learn to fly, Edwin gives Bessie the money to buy a plane at last. Gossips' tongues wag, and Edwin"s wife storms about her mansion raging about the "black slut."

Bessie arranges to have her plane, a second-hand Jenny, flown from Dallas to Jacksonville for her next big show. Just one more payday, and she will have enough to open her school.

"I've got my plane, I've got enough money, I've got my work that I love, I've got a faith I never had. Now I won't have to fly all the time to make money. I'm going to stay on the ground more and visit churches and schools and spread the word." She gives them each a big hug. "I've never been so happy in my life."

Resplendent in her full flying uniform, Bessie steps off the train in Jacksonville to be met by Behncke and Beeman. She tells Behncke how happy she is to see him, but she leaves in Beeman"s roadster while Behncke watches them go.

As their car leaves the station, they pass a park, where a Ku Klux Klan wedding is taking place. The groom, preacher, and guests all wear white robes and peaked hats.

Beeman whisks her from school to school throughout the city, where wide-eyed black kids listen raptly to her pep talks.

William Wills, a young white mechanic delivers her plane, complaining to Bessie that she got robbed. Unlike her last plane, this is second-hand. The engine kept giving him trouble the whole trip, he says, and he had to make two emergency landings for repairs. It's supposed to put out ninety horsepower, but he could only get it up to sixty.

There's a last-minute hitch: The show will be for whites only. Bessie puts her foot down. "The sky is open to everyone, and the ground should be too," she says. Otherwise she'll send her plane back to Texas and withdraw.

"No, don"t do that," the promoter begs, "we've already sold a thousand tickets." He huddles with two colleagues, and at last announces, "We'll have two grandstands, and two ticket windows."

Again Bessie protests, but the promoter shrugs that there's nothing he can do; the law in Florida says blacks and whites have to be separated. "What about the ticket windows?" she asks.

The promoters confer again. "Okay," they agree, "we'll have one ticket window and two grandstands."

Behncke and Bessie whisper. "You have to do it," he says, "if you want to get your school." At last she agrees.

Outside the fair grounds, where Bessie is being advertised, pickets carry placards:

KEEP THE SKY WHITE
SHOOT BLACKBIRDS

In a restaurant, Bessie unexpectedly meets Abbott and rushes over to kiss him on the cheek. "This is the man who gave me my start," she says. "I'll never forget him."

"I was out to the field this morning and saw your plane and the mechanic," Abbott says. "I didn't like the looks of it at all."

"He's going to be my co-pilot Saturday."

"Bessie, take the advice of an old friend: Don't fly. I just don't like the way things smell."

"Don't worry, dear," she says with another kiss, "I'll be careful. I promise."

Next morning Bessie drives to the airport for a check-out flight. She bends a knee in prayer, then climbs into the passenger seat in front and buckles on her safety belt.

"Contact."

A mechanic spins the propeller, the engine coughs and dies. He whirls again, and it sputters and catches.

Circling above, Bessie tries to look over the side, but she's too short to see. She unbuckles her seatbelt, puts one knee on the seat, and leans out.

Suddenly the old Jenny lurches forward in a nose dive. Bessie grabs the windshield and desperately fumbles for the safety belt buckle as the plane screams toward the ground.

Then it goes into a tailspin and suddenly flips onto its back. Spectators watch in horror as a small body tumbles out, falling end-over-end.

Wills fights to regain control and finally levels off but shears off the top of a tree and pancakes into the ground.

The sheriff is holding the wrench and studying the plane. "Let's take another look at that wall between the cockpit and the engine," he says, taking a step toward the fuselage.

The deputy lights a cigarette and flips the match, and suddenly the plane erupts in a fireball explosion. They hold their arms to their faces as the blast blows them backwards.

The sheriff picks himself up. "Damn," he drawls to the deputy, "we'll never know now. Write it up as an accident." He tosses the wrench aside and wipes his hands.

In a packed church in Chicago, Bessie"s coffin rests in front of the congregation. Momma, Georgia, and her many friends are in the front row. Behnke, Beeman, and other whites are scattered in the pews. The choir lifts its voices in a hymn:

"I've done my work,

I've sung my song.

I've done some good,

I've done some wrong.

And I shall go where I belong.

At the cemetery the coffin is lowered as a soloist softly sings

"Jesus Savior, pilot me

Over life's tempestuous sea...."

Above the gravesite a small plane slowly crosses the sky. Inside, two women and a man drop a large horseshoe of roses.

With the passage of time more modern planes follow, each flight dropping roses. The last flight is a jet.

At Cape Kennedy a Challenger spacecraft sits on the launch pad in the pre-dawn. **Mae Jemison,** a black astronaut, tucks Bessie's picture into her space jacket, and cradles her space helmet in her arm.

As the hymn plays, from space we see the blue ocean below. The camera descends for a closer look at angry whitecaps tossing. Next Texas cotton fields and sharecropper shacks glide below us... followed by the Chicago skyline, ghetto, and lake shore... the Paris Eiffel Tower... Florida and the field at Jacksonville... the ocean again, now tranquil, as one small biplane flies into the sunrise.

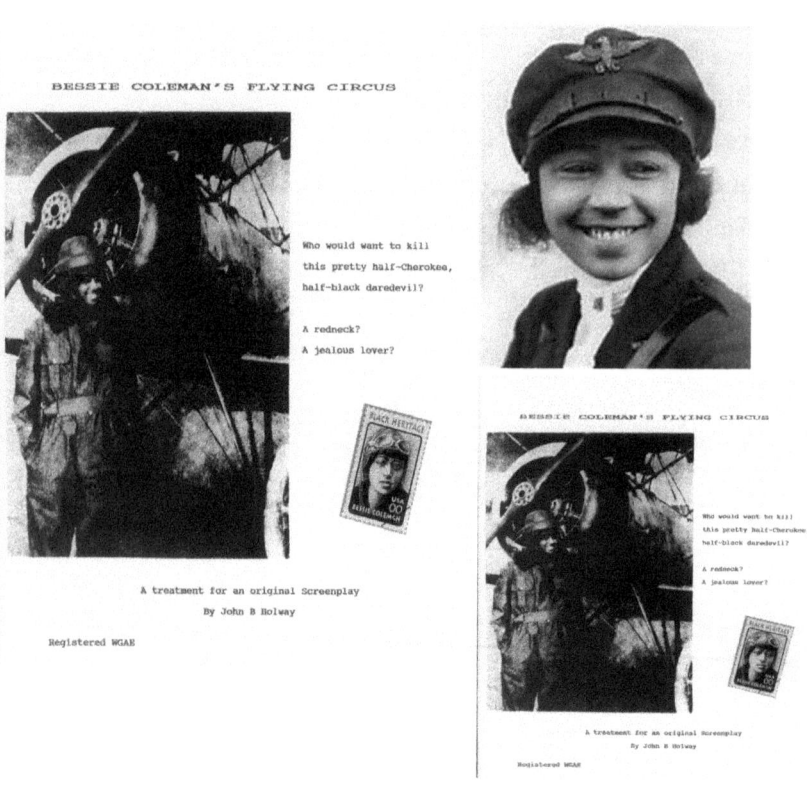

STEVE NELSON
A VALLEY IN SPAIN

AN IMMIGRANT FROM CROATIA ENDURES POLICE BEATINGS AND LEADS COAL MINERS TO VICTORY

THEN HE RISKS HIS LIFE IN AN EVEN GREATER BATTLE TO STOP FASCISM AS AMERICA SLEEPS.

A harmonica softly plays "Red River Valley" as a male voice softly sings:

> There's a valley in Spain named Jarama,
> It's a place that we all know so well,
> It was there that we wasted our manhood
> And most of our old age as well.

COAL

Croatia (Yugoslavia) 1921. A mill in the mountains. Stjepan Mesaros, 18, and his father load the family goods into a horse cart, help the women and children up, then climb onto the carts' seat, cluck to the horses, and begin a jolting, bumpy ride to the sea.

New York. Their ship passes the Statue of Liberty as they wave and point excitedly. They emerge from a subway into a madhouse of honking autos, omnibuses, and neighing horses. They show a piece of paper to a passer-by, who points uptown, and they pick up their burdens and start walking.

Detroit. They live in a crowded apartment with outdoor privy. Steve joins hundreds waiting in line for work on cold winter mornings and gets a job driving rivets with a steam hammer on an assembly line for 26 cents an hour. He joins the Communist party and with **Joe Dalat** sells the *Daily Worker* on a street corner. At party headquarters he meets Margaret, his future wife.

All Communists, along with others, are fired. Thousands of workers pack the streets around city hall, demanding higher pay, until mounted cops charge. A cry goes up: "Cossacks! Cossacks!" Steve pounds the horses' snouts until they rear and shie away.

But two detectives grab him by the hair, push him into a car, force his head between his legs, and whack him with a black jack. He passes out.

He comes to in a police station with Dalat. Steve pushed onto a chair. The cop slowly pulls out a black jack. Crack! Again and again. A kick in the ribs, and he passes out. When he comes to, Joe is sitting with others, bleeding from his mouth, a gash on his cheek, his hair caked with blood.

But only two weeks later, they are out demonstrating again, this time for unemployment insurance. Steve and Joe are arrested again and are brought into court for sedition and organizing an armed revolution. Fortunately, the jury is made up of workers, and they are acquitted **1933**. Roosevelt is elected President, and Steve's next assignment is the Pennsylvania coal mines. He and Margaret buy a jalopy for $15 for the trip, and are trailed by a car of goons (police). At a narrow bridge of planks, Steve suddenly guns the gas, the planks fly up in the air behind them, and the goons plunge into the creek.

They reach a town of shacks along a railroad track. Troops patrol the street.

They find the local labor leader, whose fingers are blue from a life-time of wounds infected with coal dust.

He invites them into his home. Inside the walls are covered with tar paper. Cracks in the walls are stuffed with newspapers or pages from Sears Roebuck catalogues. The miner invites them in for meals. "We ate a lot of potatoes and bread," Steve remembers.

He address a roomful of striking miners. While cops watch through the windows, Steve asks: "What are you going to do when you can't pay your rent?"

The miners sit silently, some with tears in their eyes.

"Let's not wait for miracles! Let's go and see the legislators and the governor and ask for food for families in need!"

Every man raises his hand - even one of the cops in the back.

Next Sunday the local pastor declares: "I must say, those miners were better Christians than some of the people in the congregation." He is promptly fired.

A caravan of cars sets out for the capital, Steve in the lead, state police on motorcycles in the rear.

At the city limit they are told they can't enter by order of Governor Pinchot.

Shout: "Let's force our way in!"

Steve: "No, it's a trap."

Joe: "We must have 3,000 people. Where we gonna put them all?"

Steve: "Let's go!"

They hop in his jalopy and head out of town. The puzzled police shrug, gun their motor cycle pedals, and follow.

At dusk they reach a Pennsylvania Dutch farmhouse, with two barns, identified by their hex signs. There's a light in the living room. The guys knock.

A man with a beard and

lantern and his wife in a night cap open the door. He holds his light up and surveys them.

"What can we possibly do for you folks?"

Steve explains.

"Uh, how many of you are there?" he asks.

"Well, uh, "Steve begins, "we didn't count, but, uh - quite a few ."

"Five hundred?"

"Er… more than that…"

His wife speaks up. "The lord sent them here, so perhaps it's up to us to help."

The farmer: "Well, mother, I think you're right."

To Steve: "But, whatever you do, be careful of fires. My insurance doesn't cover it, and I can't lose all my cattle."

They go back in the house. The light goes out.

The men hug each other, leap into their cars, and head back to the city, where the other leaders are sleeping in a garage. "Get up! We've found a place! Tell everyone to follow my Ford."

A caravan of 200 jalopies and trucks slowly disappears into the night.

When they arrive, the word is passed: "No matches!" Empty barrels are set at each barn. Men drop their smokes and file into two barns, women into the other.

In the morning coffee is brewing. The farmer comes out, climbs onto a flatbed, bows his head, raises his hands, and in a slow and quiet voice that can barely be heard, intones a prayer. He and his wife are trying not to cry. In fact, the entire group is dabbing away tears.

The men produce a blanket, lift him onto it, and toss him in the air, all laughing and crying at the same time.

Climbing into their jalopies, they wave as they chug slowly over the hill back to town.

At the city limits they dismount, and take out their signs:

WE DEMAND RELIEF, etc.

The cops watch but don't interfere, and the march begins, 20 abreast. eight blocks long, toward the capital. On-lookers join them, and here and there some state legislators step off the curb and fall in step. One drops $10 into a collection hat.

Other legislators and police wait for them, blocking the way. Steve and others step forward to parlay. They are told they can camp in the state fairgrounds. A cheer goes up. The Red Cross is already there, setting up cots, food, and blankets.

The marchers huddle and elect four speakers to meet with the lawmakers - one white, one black, one from the coal mines, one from the steel mills.

This is refused. They can have only one spokesman, and he may speak only from the gallery.

With Steve and other leaders in front, the crowd surges to the state capitol, and the galleries are quickly packed. Someone produces a rope, tie it to the gallery railing, and their spokesman slides down. The other spokesmen slide down behind him and join him in front of the Speaker's desk. More make the slide and go over to their home town legislators' desks, and quietly sit cross-legged on the floor beside them.

The lawmakers are overwhelmed. Bills to provide relief are read and approved.

SPAIN

Grainy newsreel footage shows Nazi dive bombers screaming down on Madrid . . . bombs exploding on streets and buildings below. . . civilians lying dead and bleeding in the streets. Other scenes show Italian tanks unloading in Spanish harbors . . . goose stepping troops give Fascist salutes as sullen people watch.

News from San Francisco shows students marching in protest.

In New York a German ship lies at anchor, a Nazi flag flying at its mast. Dock workers on the wharf push aside police, charge up the gangplank, haul down the flag, and tear it to shreds.

Steve, Joe, and their wives sit around a spare kitchen table with newspapers spread on it:

RED WORKERS SAIL FOR SPAIN
Defy Roosevelt's Neutrality Ban

Reading the men's minds, the women silently reach out and squeeze their hands.

At a dockside in New York, Steve and Joe, dressed unconvincingly as tourists, join others like them in a line to board a French luxury liner. At sea, they watch the New York skyline recede, try their skills in a game of shuffleboard on deck, then file into the swanky dining hall for dinner.

As the other diners sip after-dinner coffee, Joe strolls to the grand piano and plays some tentative notes, then swings into "I'm in Mood for Love," as the guests turn to listen, He segues into some bars from Beethoven's Piano Concerto and ends with a lively jazz piece, "One O'clock Jump," to applause.

"I never knew you could play," Steve says later.

"Yeah, I took lessons when I was a kid. I'm not your typical Socialist. My folks had money. We even went to Europe one summer on a ship like this."

"Jeez!" Steve says,

The ship's newspaper carries news that untrained Americans in Spain fought their first battle at a place called Jarama. They charged down a hillside to protect a vital road to Madrid. They held the road, but lost 500 dead.

In the harbor, local Reds put the "tourists" on a train to the South. France is officially neutral, and if they are caught trying to cross, it means prison.

They emerge at sunset at the foot of the Pyrenees, a daunting snow-capped range. Out of the shadows steps their guide, with a scar across his cheek. He says nothing but motions them to follow.

As shadows great deeper, the grade get steeper and narrower. The guide motions them to hug the mountain side. A Dutchman, a short, overweight man, wheezes and stumbles. He motions the others to leave him, but Steve and Joe cut two limbs with a knife and pin a blanket between them. He refuses the help, but they rub his face with snow and insist. The party goes forward.

A cry. Someone misses a step, and the sound fades away into the dark.

At last dawn breaks on a nearby peak, and the exhausted men demand a break, but the guide refuses, pointing to the sun: *Plus vite!* ("Faster!") The Dutchman climbs down and refuses more help, but two new men grab him under each shoulder. He wheezes but limps to keep up.

They turn a corner and sight a guard shack.

"*Espana!*" the guide says.

Everyone forgets his fatigue and begins to half-run and half-stumble, falling to the ground around the shack, laughing and gasping.

At last someone softly someone begins singing the *Internationale*:

Stand up, victims of oppression...

One by one, they totter to their feet, and join in in various languages:

For the tyrants fear your might.
Don't cling to your possessions.
You have none without your rights.

Then they sprawl back, gasping and laughing, on the ground.

At the foot the mountain, Steve gets a military uniform out of his pack, smoothes it out, and climbs aboard a truck to Jarama.

The newcomers are welcomed by a rabble of American poets, professors, and labor leaders, still recovering from Jarama.

One man points with his chin to a ridge: "The Fascists - over there."

Steve and Joe jump off at a cave entrance. A man is playing "Red River Valley" on a harmonica. Others hum.

They peer inside. A black man is sitting on the floor, his back against the wall. He gets up and extends his hand: "Hi, I'm Law - **Oliver Law**. I've heard all about you. Glad to have you with us."

Steve snaps an awkward salute. "And I've heard about you - Chicago's South Side. You were in the Army in France, right?"

Law gives them a casual one-finger salute in return and nods. "And this is our commissar - our number-two man - **Merriman**," pointing to a tall pipe-smoking man next to him. They shake. "They're kicking him upstairs to regiment, so you got here just in time. You're his replacement, Nelson."

"His *what*?!"

Merriman laughs. "You'll learn fast. Three months ago I was teaching English at UCLA."

Three shells explode. Law glances at his watch: "Nine o'clock. Right on time." When all is quiet again, He laughs. "They do it every night. It's our alarm clock. You can set your watch by it. They won't do it again until tomorrow morning, so we can take you for a look at our lines now."

At the hospital they meet ambulance driver Evelyn Hutchins and wounded survivors of Jarama.

They arrive at the mess line, where cook Jackie Shirai, a sawed-off little Nissei, is protesting. "How are you, old timer?" Steve greets him.

"No more kitchen for me! I came here to shoot Fascists!" He brandishes his Russian rifle.

They smile and walk on. "It's your call now, Commissar!" Merriman chuckles. "He's the only good cook we've got."

"Who's the worst one?"

"Hmmm. I guess Dombrowski.

Steve walks back: "Dombrowski, let's see how good you can cook breakfast."

Next morning the men are retching, spitting, and scraping their mess tins into the garbage. Especially Shirai.

Steve strolls up and listens. "How about it, Jack? If you'll come back, I promise you can go on every attack." The guys cheer.

Segue to guys drilling, taking target practice, playing ball with kids, dolling out pills, pitching in to harvest the barley, flirting with the girls.

They also go on R&R to **Ernest Hemingway**'s hotel suite in Madrid, well stocked with booze and pretty girls.

Law calls a meeting of officers and spreads a map. "Here's the next place we hit - Bruneet - or Brunete - whatever they call it."

At dawn sergeants go from room to room, banging on doors. Sleepy-eyed men line up at their trucks, Jackie among them. He tries twice to pull himself up onto the truck bed, and Law gives him a friendly slap of the rear end. He backs up, dusts his hands, makes a run, and gets his torso in while wildly kicking his feet. Friendly hands reach for his collar and pants and pull him in.

The trucks chug off as townspeople follow, shouting, "*Viva La Republica! Viva Americanos!*"

A square in the town. The guys jump down from their trucks as townspeople come around a corner, led by a little girl with flowers. Suddenly Fascist soldiers appear behind them and open fire. Many in the crowd are hit; the rest scatter. Some *Americanos* also go down, the others quickly un-shoulder their own weapons, load, and fire back.

Soon, silence. The square is littered with bodies. One is the little girl, the flowers lying beside her outstretched hand.

The Lincolns keep going to Mosquito Ridge, alongside eight small Italian tanks. Above them, German Heinkel dive bombers scream down.

With a cheer they wade across a stream and head uphill, firing as they go, as Law waves them on with his pistol. Someone begins singing "the Internationale;" the rest join in.

Law waves them on with his pistol until machine gun slugs tear into his stomach. He is carried off. Within an hour he is dead.

Steve now commands the brigade.

At the top, the Americans fire from behind a wall.

The Division commander, Nathan, arrives and patrols the line under heavy fire, calmly swinging a swagger stick, his pipe cocked at a jaunty angle.

Dusk. Men sleep on their arms. A new order arrives - march nine miles back to relieve a Spanish division that is surrounded.

"Impossible!" Joe says. "They marched nine miles to get *here*! They're exhausted."

Nathan: "What will we do?"

Steve: "If the order is explained to the men, I think they'll go back. And if the Americans go, I think the rest will follow."

He calls his men together. They grumble, slowly rub their eyes, and gather around. From the top of a rock, Steve reads the order.

"My God, Steve," comes a voice from the rear. "You're not telling us to go *back*?!"

Steve: "I have no more pep left than you. But there are three thousand comrades surrounded by Fascists, and we do nothing to help? Besides, we have no chance to hold the line here."

Voice: "You're telling us to do the impossible!"

Steve: "It's our job to do the impossible. This is impossible time."

Silence.

Then a voice from the rear: "You're right."

No one else speaks.

Steve to Nathan: "I think the decision has been made."

Belchite - their next objective, on the road to Barcelona. It's strongly defended. It can't be taken - even Napoleon failed to take it. But it *must* be taken: If they go around, they'll leave a dangerous force in their rear.

A New York *Herald-Tribune* reporter, James Lardner, son of the humorist, gets so excited he drops his typewriter and picks up a rifle.

Jarama. Moving by night into a shallow trench, the men creep toward the church, where the Germans had set up machine gunners in the belfry. Any man who lifts his head six inches will get a bullet through it.

Dawn breaks, which means a long, hot day ahead. "We have to go forward," Steve says, "but that's impossible. And retreat over bare ground will cost more lives than an attack."

It's his job to find a solution.

With Joe Dalat and Joe Carter, he crawls along the ditch to an olive oil factory next to the church. At Steve's signal they lob grenades through a window, then rush in. Luckily it's empty. They set up machine guns.

They have a foothold in town!

But the enemy still holds the church and commands the streets that run from it like spokes.

More Lincs arrive. They can't use the streets, so they have to clear every house. They shout, "Open!" but when they are met with machine gun fire, they drop the "Open!" command and simply kick each door in, then bust through the walls and clear the next house.

Steve starts back to the factory. "Steve, look out!" Joe cries.

"Something hard hit me in the cheek," he remembers. "A fierce pain in my thigh ran up to my stomach." He doubles over and rolls toward a brick wall for safety.

Hands cut his clothes away and press on the wound to stop the bleeding. Dalat and Carter lift him onto a stretcher.

A dim, wildly swinging room. Distant sounds of artillery. A man groans and calls for help. Slowly the room stops reeling. Two long lines of beds emerge, each with a body covered with sheets.

Steve painfully sits up. Six stretchers are brought in, carrying men drenched in blood. Next to him a man lies and calls for help.

Joe Dalat lies on the other side with unseeing eyes open, gasping for breath. Nurses bend over him. He begs for water, recognizes Steve, and reaches out. They touch hands. "Did we take the town?" Steve whispers. Joe nods. Then he drops his hand, and a nurse pulls the sheet over him.

In the town battered volunteers watch Fascist soldiers file out with hands upraised. One man moves among them with a mail sack, calling names. Some voices respond and claim their letters. Other names provoke no answers. One of the latter is Lardner.

A Paris hotel. Steve, on crutches, stands as Joe's wife, Kitty, emerges from an elevator and runs happily to him. They embrace. Then she sags, and he has to catch her.

Back Home. Steve speaks at a podium: "Half of the volunteers who went to Spain are buried there. Half the Fascists' oil and trucks come from the United States. If we can convince our government to shut off that aid, the struggle can be won! If not, we'll have to face the Fascists again in other places and in other times!"

Scattered boos are mixed with cheers.

All the foreign volunteers are sent home. But the German and Italian tanks and bombers remain. The Republic falls; the Fascists triumph. Lardner is one who does not answer his name at mail call. Many who return are battered by police. and hounded as "PAFs" - Premature Anti-Fascists.

After Pearl Harbor asome veterans from Spain join the U.S. Army - Joe Carter is one - and are hounded as "PAFs" - Premature Anti-Fascists. Carter wins the Medal of Honor.

After the war. Nelson is indicted for trying to steal atomic secrets and send them to Russia. No lawyer will take the case. He defends himself and is sentenced to 20 years in prison. The conviction is over-turned by the Supreme Court.

In 1986, Nelson, now 83, returns to Spain with other vets to walk the old battlefields and receive the kisses and hugs of the people.

The harmonica softly plays "Red River Valley" as Hemingway intones:

> *The dead sleep cold in Spain tonight. Snow blows through the olive groves, sifting against the tree roots. Snow blows over the mounds with small headboards (if there was time for headboards) .... The dead are part of the earth now. And the earth can never be conquered.*

ACE OF
DIAMONDS

FROM FIGHTER PILOT TO THE BIG LEAGUES.
ON ONE LEG

IN APRIL 1944 LT BERT SHEPARD WALKS OFF A BASEBALL DIAMOND IN ENGLAND, STRAPS HIMSELF INTO A P-38 FIGHTER PLANE, AND ROARS INTO THE SKIES OVER AUSTRIA.

IN APRIL 1945 HE WALKS OUT OF WALTER REED HOSPITAL, STRAPS ON AN ARTIFICIAL LEG, AND RUNS OUT TO PITCH IN A MAJOR LEAGUE GAME.

Baseball dugout. Bert Shepard hops into the field, "8th Air Force" blazoned on his uniform, and trots to the mound, giving a wave to a pretty girl, June, in the stands, who waves back.

The inning ends with a strikeout, and a sergeant is waiting. "Sir, the colonel wants to see you. They're short one pilot, and he wants you suit up as fast as you can."

"Damn," Bert says, "I flew yesterday." He smiles: "I know, I know - 'There's a war on.' OK. I can be back before the game is over." He gives June a quick kiss, vaults the fence, and trots to his barracks, stripping off his baseball shirt as he goes.

The flight line. Bert climbs into his P-38 cockpit, give a wave to his crew chief, and taxi onto the flight line behind other planes impatiently gunning their throttles. Then he's off. He circles the field and dips his wings. June gives a big wave back and blows a kiss.

The plane disappears into a cloud.

A 1930s rural Indiana high school. Kids pour out the door. They clamber onto a school bus, but young Bert trots past them to the baseball diamond. He's the youngest kid there and hangs out, hoping to play catch with the bigger varsity boys.

Dusk. Darkness has descended, and the team gathers its bats and gloves and troops into the locker room. Bert slings his books over his shoulder with a strap and trots toward home. Night has fallen when he jogs to a farmhouse. He goes to the oven, finds his dinner, and hungrily eats.

Farmhouse. Bert knocks at the kitchen door, and a mop-headed kid opens it. "Looks like I shoulda come last week," Bert jokes, tousling the boy's hair. The boy leads him to the kitchen table, and Bert pulls a scissors and comb from his overalls pocket and goes to work. Five other boys, each a little taller than the next, wait their turns. Finally, Dad sits down for a trim and counts six dimes into Bert's hand.

The family waves as he heads home, stopping at a drug store for a chocolate soda for a dime. At home, he hands the other five to his mother.

A forest workers' camp. A strapping, grown up Bert is working as a lumberjack in a Roosevelt-era work program.

Beside a railroad. Bert hops a freight train, and hitch-hikes to Wisconsin.

A minor league field. He vaults over the bullpen fence and trots to the mound past five or six local girls in the stands, who wave and call out.

Bert takes an old-fashioned windmill windup, stops at the top, kicks high, and pitches. The first batter singles through the infield.

The manager walks out. "Keep it on the corners," he says. "Don't give him anything good to hit, but don't walk him."

The next four pitches are close, but the ump calls all four of them balls. The manager walks to the mound and grumbles, "Damn it! I told you not to walk him."

Three more balls to the next batter. Bert leaves the next pitch too close to the center of the plate, and the batter hits it down the first-base line. Men on first and third.

"Damn it, I told you not to give 'im anything to hit," the manager growls.

The third hitter bunts. Bert springs off the mound, pounces on it, and fires home. Out.

But after two balls the next man doubles, and two runs score.

"I thought I told you to keep it on the corners," the manager says in the dugout.

"I did, but the ump won't give me the corners."

Beer joint. Bert hands his bottle to his date, chalks his cue, and breaks the rack. His opponent, Gerry, sinks the #2 ball. Bert pockets #11 and 13. Gerry misses his shot. Bert studies the table and sinks four more. At last the 8-ball is left. Bert banks a shot into the corner pocket.

Gerry, his wedding band showing, opens his wallet and hands Bert a crinkled ten-dollar bill. Bert goes back to his beer and his girl. "One more," Gerry says.

"Naw, that's enough for tonight," Bert replies.

"I'll play ya," a local shark tells Gerry, moving toward the table.

Bert turns and retrieves his cue. "OK," he says to Gerry, "one more."

Bert faces a tough shot. The 8-ball blocks the pocket, but Bert neatly hits his ball past it to the rail and into the pocket. Then he runs the rest of the table. Gerry pulls his last ten-spot from the wallet.

Bert sees Gerry move through the crowd to the exit. "Be right back," he tells his date.

"Here," he says, handing the two bills back. Gerry protests. "Go ahead. That's the rent money, right?" He pushes the bills into Gerry's hand. "Those sharks in there would have cleaned you out. Do me a favor, OK? Don't come back."

Back at the ball field, Bert pitches and winces. "How's the wing?" his manager asks.

"OK," Bert says bravely.

"Ready to pitch again tonight?"

"Sure."

"That'll be three games the week. Sure you don't mind?"

"No, I'm fine."

Manager's office. The arm hasn't improved, they're going to have to let him go. He shakes hands and slowly walks out the door.

World War II flight line. Five cadets stand diffidently with unaccustomed parachutes on their backs. The lieutenant is going down the line. "You ever flown before?"

Each one nods, "Yes, sir".... "A little."

"At a county fair once," drawls Tom Penn, a 6'2" 210-pound cowboy.

The instructor comes to Shepard.

Bert grins. "Sir, I've never been within five miles of a plane in my life."

The instructor rolls his eyes. "OK, I'll take you first."

Bert straps himself into the cockpit.

In the air. The instructor lets him hold the controls, shows him how to pull gently back on the stick to go up, how to push forward to go down. Bert pulls back, the nose goes up, and the plane almost stalls. He pushes too much and almost goes into a dive as the instructor grabs the stick. Bert is having a ball, yelling into the wind.

On the ground he climbs out, his eyes wide with excitement. "Wow! That's the greatest feeling in the world!"

"You mean the second greatest," Penn laughs.

Next day. A new instructor reads from a clipboard. "Cadet Shepard!" Bert climbs into the cockpit. "OK," the instructor says, "take off."

"Take off!?" Bert mumbles to himself. "I've never even touched the controls." But he grips the wheel, and the plane lurches forward. It swerves sharply to the left. He wrenches the controls to the right. The plane veers crazily to the right. He compensates to the left again. The plane does S-curves back and forth down the runway.

The end of the runway. A row of trees rises. As on-lookers grit their teeth or hide their eyes, the wheels slowly rise and skim the treetops.

On landing. They watch as Bert's plane starts down short of the runway and lifts off for another try. Then he comes in long and lifts off again. Finally, he touches down, bounces up, slams down, and bounces again as Penn and the others scatter. Shep brakes to a stop inches from a stone wall.

Bert and the shaken instructor climb out.

"Heh," Bert cries, "I think I'm getting the hang of it."

Advanced training. "Today we'll practice spins," the lieutenant announces. Tom goes up first, and they watch as the plane behaves erratically. "Something wrong with this bird," he says as he climbs out and Bert climbs in.

In the air. Bert puts it into a spin to the left. When he tries to pull out to the right, it doesn't respond but continues spiraling down. The ground spins up rapidly, rushing up closer and closer. A long shot shows how low he is getting.

"Right rudder! Right rudder!" Penn shouts from the ground.

Bert fights the controls. Slowly the spinning stops, the nose comes slowly up, he skims some trees and brings it in. "Better check the trim on that damn thing," he mutters to the instructor as he walks away.

Night. New wings on his chest and a new gold bar on his collar, Bert is cruisng in a P-38, the distinctive fighter with the cockpit set between twin engines, each with its separate tail boom. He watches the California coast below and the city of San Francisco ahead in the distance. A fog bank rolls in, and in barely an instant he can't see anything. He picks up the radio and reports.

A voice crackles back. "Go on up to San Francisco and try to find a place to land."

"It looks just as bad up there too."

"Well, then, fly out over the Bay and ditch it. We'll pick you up in the morning. Just be careful of the mountains. Over and out."

"Ditch it?... Mountains?... Morning!" Bert cusses under the drone of the engines. "That's a bunch of crap - I'd be shark food by morning. What mountains? I can't see a damn thing!"

Bert keeps one eye on the compass, the other on the sinking fuel gauge and squints through the black clouds. There's a brief opening, and a light twinkles. He heads toward it.

As he approaches, he makes out an open hangar door with a plane inside, nestled in a ring of mountains. He comes down and crosses the field, searching for the runway but can't find it. He circles for another look.

On the ground. A Navy ensign scrambles his anti-aircraft gunners: "Unidentified plane coming in."

"Japs?" someone shouts.

The men spring to their .50-calibre guns and aim them skyward, swinging them to follow the roar of Shepard's engines. His ship appears out of the fog, giving the defenders a quick glimpse of his Air Force insignia.

As Shepard brings his plane in, sailors rush out to him. After handshakes, they give him a chance to wash up, then invite him to the dance. **Dance hall.** Bert dreamily clasps a girl and sways to Glenn Miller's "String of Pearls." The ensign taps him on the shoulder. "Did you know you almost got shot down out there?" Bert smiles and spins the girl away.

Next morning. More handshakes as Bert climbs into the cockpit for the flight home. A four-stripe Navy captain comes up. "Heh, Air Force, can you give us a 'buzz job?'"

"Hot damn!" Bert grins. "That's like askin' me can I eat more ice cream!" He snaps a salute and starts the engine.

He climbs high to gain altitude, then turns the nose down to gain speed, levels out, almost touching the grass. He roars past the control tower at 350 miles an hour. The guys in the tower cheer as he streaks past below their eye level. On the run-way the waving sailors lose their hats in a swirl of dust and wind. As Shep climbs and turns to the left, he looks back and grins.

Back at base. the colonel calls him in and puts him at ease. "Shep," he says, "if any of my boys gets hit in combat, I sure hope it's you" - Bert looks quizzical - "I think you're the one that could handle it."

England. A rainy winter's day. Bert takes off to test his new P-38 and disappears above the clouds. His altimeter reads 39,000 feet. Then 39,500. He points the nose up, but the plane falls off to the left. It wallows in the sky. "Uh-oh, air's too thin," he mutters. He tries to bank to the right, but the plane doesn't respond. "Better get airspeed fast."

Bert pushes the stick forward, and the plane dives. We watch the ground get closer and closer. As the plane gains speed, the ground rushes up faster. "Not yet," he says to himself, "a little more." Trees and buildings take shape and grow quickly in size. "Now!" he says, and pulls back on the stick. The plane responds and slowly levels off.

Next day. Bert goes up again. This time the plane pulls to the right - one propeller isn't functioning. "Damn, it's running away from me." The elevator flap on one wing moves, correcting it. But it still pulls. The vertical tail flap moves on command, and the plane straightens out.

As he comes in for the landing, red lights erupt on his control panel. "What the hell...? There's so many lights, I don't know what they all are.... Uh-oh, landing gear malfunction."

He tries to put the gear down, but the lights won't go off. Well, there's only two ways to get down - I can try to belly land, or they can shoot me down." Grimly he makes his final approach turn and comes in for a touch down. As the runway rushes to meet him, we can see what he can't - the wheels are down. The landing is perfect.

Bert pulls off his helmet and climbs out as his mechanic trots up. "The prop ran away from me," Bert says, "then the landing gear warning lights and everything else started blinking. What the hell's going on?"

"I dunno," the mechanic shrugs. "This is the first P-38 I've ever worked on" – Bert raises his eyebrows – "but I'm studying the manual at night."

"That's good," Shep says dryly, rolling his eyes.

Beneath winter clouds. Bert and Tom are ready for their first combat mission. The operations officer stands before a huge map of Europe and slaps his pointer on Berlin. You'll rendezvous with the bombers at 0945 here" - he slaps. "You can expect heavy anti-aircraft here" - he slaps the map again.

The flight-line. Shep admits to butterflies. "Well, let's get going across the Pisser," Tom says to break the tension.
"The what?"
"The Pisser - the Channel."
They climb into their planes and bump down the field and into the air.

Aloft. They spot the bomber armada, and the fighters climb to 30,000 feet to provide top cover. They're higher than Mount Everest, and his temperature gauge shows minus 30 degrees in the cockpit. Bert's teeth are chattering. He reaches for a hose bringing warm air from one of the engines and shoves the hose into his left mitten, then into his right, and one by one into each of his boots.

German fighters appear at 11 o'clock. Bert's wing commander signals him and peels off into the attackers, Bert right behind. Their nose cannons spit tracers at the approaching enemy, who turn away. The two Americans rejoin the armada, and all fly on.

Flak blossoms like huge black donuts in the air around them. Bert's plane is buffeted by the blasts. He holds course.

Bert spots a B-17 "Flying Fortress" bomber that has fallen behind the others. He peels off to provide protection. He looks it over. "Engines all working OK," he muses. He moves in closer. "No holes in the fuselage.... Are they crazy? They're heading toward Switzerland." The tail gunner and waist gunners wave and flash smiles. He watches as the big bomber lumbers toward the frontier. The war is over for them. Shep shrugs and rejoins his squadron.

Back at the base, The pilots slowly climb out. Some limp on frost-bitten feet and wince if someone touches their hands. Seven are helped onto stretchers and carried off the field.

A theater in town. Bert, Tom, and others head inside.

A comedian finishes his routine and exits as a chorus line of high-kicking girls dances on stage. Whistles and clapping from the audience, Bert joining in enthusiastically.

His eye picks out the prettiest girl, June, on the end. He winks. She looks puzzled. He nods: "Yes, you." She smiles back. He grins broadly. She tosses her head. He blows a kiss. She is flustered. Tom suddenly understands what is going on and looks quickly at Bert, who is describing a circle with one finger: "Let's go dancing." As the line kicks its way off stage, June looks back, tosses her head, and winks.

Squadron briefing room. The colonel stands before a large wall map, briefing the pilots on a night mission over Germany. "It'll be tough," he admits.

"Tough?" Tom's voice booms out from the back as everyone swings around to look at him. "It'll be like going into a pitch-dark cave and tryin' to screw a hungry grizzly bear!"

From his plane, Bert sees a P-38 below with a Messerchmitt on his tail pumping bullets at him. Bert rolls over and heads down to join the fight. Seeing him, the enemy pilot breaks off and flies away.

German planes are spotted at two o'clock, heading toward the bombers. Bert and Tom turn toward them, but the Germans veer away.

At the base officers' club, Bert, June, Tom, and his date line up at the punch bowl. The colonel arrives with a pretty girl and a bandage around his head. "What happened, Colonel?" Tom asks. "She run under the bed on you?" The colonel shoots him a dirty look.

A dance floor. The lights are low, and mirrors on a revolving ball send constellations around the ceiling and the dancers as Bert and June dreamily dance to "I'm in the Mood for Love." As the last notes drift away, Bert bends her into a long, low dip, and she relaxes.

In the air. A strafing mission, hitting German oil storage areas, which blow up in giant fireballs. They spot a train. Tom takes the last car, Bert takes the engine, and they roar in low, dropping their bombs as they are almost on the train. The explosions throw up a cloud of jagged metal pieces that Bert flies straight into.

His right engine is knocked out. Desperately he nurses the other one as the plane loses altitude and falls behind the fast-disappearing tails of the others. Half-gliding, he approaches the Channel, low enough to see the whitecaps below. Tom's voice breaks over the radio. "Heh, Bert, where you at? I want to come over there and watch you fall in the Pisser!"

Situation room, Girls in head phones monitor the flyers' messages and type what they hear. One girl suddenly laughs. The others look at her as she points to what she's typed. They put their hands to their mouths to hide the titters.

Squadron day room. A rest day. The pilots lounge . "I'm bored," Bert says, "I'm going up for a little spin."
Looking down at the field, he descends and does three rolls almost on the ground.

Colonel's office. "Get Shepard in here!" the Of Man barks.
"That was a fool dangerous stunt you pulled!" he chews out Bert, who is standing at attention.

Officers' baracks. "How'd it go?" Tom asks.

"I'm grounded," Bert says. "But I'm not worried. We've got too many missions coming up, and I can smell something big in the air, like the invasion. Those old farts don't want to fly too many missions. They're going to need me."

The colonel calls him in. "I can't have you laying around on your bunk doing nothing. Get your ass to the briefing in the morning. I'm sending you up."

Spring. Apple blossoms bloom around the airfield and the baseball diamond.

Burt's quarters. A phone rings' It's June. "Are you're all right?"

"Sure, I'm all right."

"I had this dream that you got shot down."

"Oh, hell, don't worry about me. Of course I'll be all right. I'll pick you up right after church Sunday for the game."

The diamond. Bert and other players are warming up. "Thirty-three missions," Tom says, tossing the ball to Bert. "Seventeen more, and we get a ticket home."

The sergeant approaches with the message from the colonel. . . .

Back in the plane. The clouds part, and the planes and their bombers fly deeper over Germany, the anti-aircraft fire gets thicker. One bomber spirals to the ground. Another loses a wing, but only one man bails out.

"Jump! Jump! Bert shrieks. Two, three, four more chutes blossom open. "Where's the other six?" he mutters. "Jump!" he shrieks. But there are no more chutes.

Another plane explodes in mid-air.

The squadron finishes its mission and rolls out to return home.

Ahead Bert spots a column of black smoke billowing up from an airfield. Several German planes have been destroyed on the ground and are burning. Several more sit unharmed. Bert changes course and heads toward the smoke, dropping down to only 20 feet to strafe before climbing back to altitude. The fire from the ground is intense. His plane shudders with each boom.

A bullet tears up through the floor and whines out the ceiling. Blood gushes out of his leg, spattering his pants and the sides of the cockpit. He looks down at his right foot, which is almost off. He reaches for the boot and slowly begins pulling his foot off.

Bert reaches for the radio. "Purple One," he calls, "this is Purple Six. My right leg is shot off."

The answer is an inaudible crackle.

"I'm going to head back. I think I can make it. I'll climb to altitude, where it's colder, and the bleeding will stop. I can fly with one foot. I'll let you know…."

A thunderous blast rocks the cockpit. Metal slivers fly in all directions. Blood spurts from Bert's chin.

Everything goes black.

Bert's wrecked plane smolders in a field. His body is inert in the wreckage. Two German planes smolder nearby. An Austrian doctor, Loidel, struggles to extract the pilots and lays them on the ground.

Austrian farmers, shouting and brandishing pitchforks, rush toward Bert's plane.

The doctor runs over, ordering them back. They shove him aside. He pulls his pistol from its holster and holds them at bay. They grudgingly retreat.

Loidel grabs Bert's unconscious form tightly and heaves. No good. He gets a tighter grip and pulls with all his might. The body moves a bit. Getting an even better hold, he locks his hands on Bert's chest and grunts. The body comes free and they both tumble onto the ground.

The doctor staunches the blood, rolls Bert onto a stretcher, and barks an order to a farmer. Together they carry Bert to an ambulance.

A farmhouse. the doctor dashes in and telephones. A German shakes his head. (Subtitle) *"He can't come here. He's a 'Terror Flier.' Take him to Badworst hospital."*

Doctor (subtitle): *"That's 30 miles away. He won't live that long."*

The officer slams the receiver down.

Loidel cranks the phone again. A German general is on the other end. He listens. Loidel talks fast. The general nods.

The screen is dark.

A hospital room swims into Bert's consciousness, German signs on the walls. Several doctors and nurses hover over Bert, who can't understand them. "Is this Heaven?" he wonders. "I've never been to Heaven, so I don't know."

Bert's chin is bandaged. He rubs it. He feels a hole and pokes his finger into it.

As his mind focuses, he looks down at the bed. A board under the sheets holds the covers off his feet. He slowly lifts the covers and looks.

As the camera pulls back, the contour of the blanket reveals that half of one leg is missing

The doctors and nurses exchange alarmed looks. They stare as the covers are slowly raised.

Bert looks up at them. He squeezes his eyes shut, tears form, his face contorts, he gropes for a nurse's hand and squeezes. He sobs.

"Thank you... Thank you. Thank you for saving my life."

They all cry and laugh together.

POW camp. Bert sits on his bunk, dangling his legs. A few knowing winks from the other POWs as a Canadian, **Don Errey**, comes in with a twinkle in his eye. "I've got something for you, Yank," he says, "a little something I whipped up in woodworking shop, plus a few pieces of scrap metal." From behind his back he pulls an artificial leg. "Ta-*DA!*"

The others burst into applause.

"Here, let's see if it fits."

Everyone gathers around as Don and Bert fit the leg to the stump and strap it on. Bert stands and tests his weight. He's a little wobbly and keeps one hand on the bunk. He winces and slowly lets go. He sways and goes down. Hands reach to help him up, but he waves them away and pulls himself up.

The leg buckles again, but he catches himself before falling. Bert grits his teeth and slowly takes one hand away. Then the other. He can stand! More applause.

He tries a step and grabs the bunk again. Then another step unaided. "Not bad," he grins. He starts to walk across the room, goes three steps and falters. Several men start to spring to his aid, but Don motions them away. Burt straightens up and resumes. Two more steps, and he lurches to a table, breathing hard but smiling.

"Pretty good," he says. "Let's see if I can get back." He turns and, stiff-legged, clumps slowly back to his bunk.

"By God, Don, I think you've done it!" He tries a dance step, but grabs the bunk as everyone cheers.

The chow line. Bert takes slow careful steps along the counter. The rest of the guys pretend not to notice. The mess sergeant does a double-take. "Lieutenant Shepard?!"

"Yeah, what is it, Sarge?"

"You're w-walking!"

"Am I gonna get any chow?" Bert says, "Or do I have to go back in the kitchen and get it myself?"

The exercise yard.. The guys draw a line in the dirt. Bert toes the line, Errey holds a stop watch and hollers, "Go!" There is a cheer as Bert lumbers off, stiff, at a slow trot, to the barracks and back. "Twenty-two-point-seven," Errey announces. "A world record - for the two hundred. But a little slow for the four-forty."

Later. Bert runs the same course a little faster.

Still later. He's almost at full speed.

The barracks. Bert is lounging on his bunk when Errey approaches. "Heh, Yank," he says, "there's a guy wants to know if you think you can still throw a baseball."

Outside,. Joe is tossing a ball in the air with one hand. "Look what the Red Cross brought us." He tosses the ball to Bert.

Burt: "Heh, I'm a little rusty."

Joe backs up, puts on a catcher's mitt and squats. The others gather around as Bert goes into his windup and lobs one way over Joe's head.

Bert goes into another windmill windup, and a lazy toss hits the mitt. "Come on," Joe urges, "put something on it." Everyone claps.

The next pitch hits the mitt with a pop. "Come on, let's see a little more mustard."

Bert takes a deep breath, winds up, kicks his leg high, and delivers with a grunt.

The ball sails straight at Joe, hits him squarely between the eyes, and bounces into the air. Joe's eyes roll back into his head, and he falls backward, out cold. Bert is alarmed and rushes to Joe's aid while everyone gathers around, waving towels and slapping Joe's face.

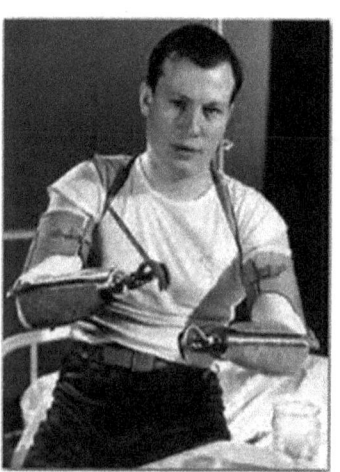

"Gee," whistles Errey, "It's a good thing you didn't throw him your *fast* ball."

A ship's rail. Bert is among wounded Americans being exchanged for wounded German POWs as it glides past the Statue of Liberty.

The Pentagon. Under-Secretary of War **Robert Patterson** rises from his desk to greet Shepard and other handicapped vets, including Oscar-winner **Harold Russell**, who has lost both hands. "So what are your plans now?" Patterson asks Bert.

"Well, sir, if I can't fly, I'd like to play baseball."

Patterson is incredulous. "Can you *do* that?"

"Yes, sir, I think I can."

After Bert leaves, the Secretary picks up the phone. "Get me Clark Griffith, the owner of the Washington Senators.... Clark? I think I've got a prospect for you."

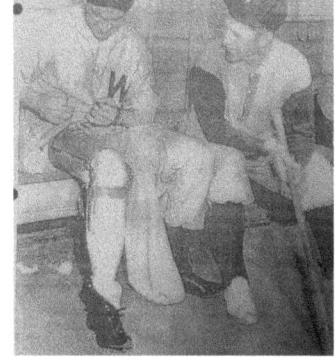

Walter Reed Hospital. Two days later Bert in civvies walks down the steps, gets in a cab, and emerges at a ballpark. The players are already on the field tossing the ball.

The clubhouse. Shep finds an empty locker, and slowly begins to change. He peels off his trousers, dons his uniform, pulls his sock up, and laces his shoe. He stands, tries on his Washington Senators cap, stops to admire it in a mirror, then clumps out.

On the field. He stands round diffidently. Two players, **Chick and Bingo**, are tossing a ball and throw one his way, including him in their group. "Shepard," he says to the man next to him, a short left-hander. "Pieretti," the other replies.

"Not Chick Pieretti?" Shep asks. "El Paso, 1942?"

"Yeah, how'd you know?

"I pitched for Bisbee."

"So where've you been since then?"

"Oh, I went in the Service."

Manager **Ossie Bluege** strolls over and nods. "You the new pitcher?"

Shep nods. "Bert Shepard."

"Oh, yeah, the guy with the wooden leg."

Bert nods again as Chick and Bingo do double-takes.

"How's it feeling?"

"Not bad."

"Want to toss a little batting practice?"

"Sure." He jogs to the pitching mound. The players stop to watch as Bert lobs a few warm-ups. One by one the other players also hear the buzz and turn to look. Bert nods that he's ready, and the batter steps in. Bert motions fastball and fires. Then he signals curve and throws again.

Pounds Haight, a bubbly, overweight writer for the Washington *Post*,

nudges Bluege. "Who's the new guy?"

"Bert Shepard. Got only one leg."

"Huh!? How come?"

"Got it shot off in the war, I think."

"He *did!*?"

Haight trots, puffing, to the clubhouse and calls his office.

Shep gives up a single. The next man bunts, and Bert is on it like a hawk and throws him out.

Several **photographers and reporters** pile out of a car and head for the field. Bert is surrounded.

"Heh, Ossie, let him hit a few," the reporters plead.

Bert shrugs, smiles,

picks up a bat, and takes a left-handed stance. He hits a weak foul down the third-base line. He misses the next one, a dancing knuckle ball, and swings late on a fastball. "It's been a few years," he apologizes.

"Pitchers can't hit," they laugh good-naturedly.

The fourth pitch he pulls into rightfield to a smattering of clapping.

"Can you run?" they ask.

Why not?"

He drops a bunt and sprints to first before the throw gets there. Then he lights out on a steal of second, sliding in with his spikes up, clipping shortstop **Hollis Layne** in the shin. Layne hops in pain: "Heh, no fair! He's got a wooden leg!"

The press follows Bert back into the clubhouse for pictures and more interviews. "How come you're so fast fielding a bunt?"

Heck," he shrugs, "anticipate. It's quickness, not speed."

"Heh, fellas," complains Layne, "Why don't you interview me?" He limps around in his shorts with one leg that is shorter than the other.

Bert carefully unrolls his socks, which are spotted with blood, un-straps his false leg, and slowly lifts it off. The skin is red and raw.

"Gee, that must hurt," Bingo winces.

"Nah, it looks worse than it is. The army doctors gave me a damn good fit. I put it on four days ago, and today I'm playing baseball. Not bad, huh?"

The season begins, but Bert rides the bench. He poses for pictures with the **Pete Gray**, the one-armed outfielder of the St Louis Browns. Gray demonstrates how he catches the ball, lets it roll into the crook of his elbow, drops his glove, lets the ball roll back, and throws, in one quick, fluid motion.

At the Washington airport, Bert, with flowers, watches a C-47 land and taxi. The door opens, and a line of women with suitcases emerge and struggle down the ramp. One of them is June. The guys burst through their restraining rope, and soon Burt and June are exchanging pent-up kisses.

In the locker room Bluege asks, "How'd you like to pitch against the Dodgers next week?"

"Sure."

"Good. We're playing an exhibition for the war bond drive. You pitch the first three innings."

Coach **Nick Altrock**, a veteran of 40 years, sidles up to the manager. "I don't know," he says, "if you let Sheppard play, you may end up with a pitcher in the hospital with a bum leg."

Game night. A big crowd is in the stands. The Marine band plays. **Leo Durocher,** the Brooklyn manager, chats with his players in the dugout. "Should we bunt on this guy, Leo?" asks Eddie Stanky, the pepper-pot second baseman.

"Hell, no," says Leo, "this will be a good chance to tee off. I want to see you guys swing those bats."

A radio announcer interrupts. "Leo, can we get an interview with you and Shepard?"

"Sure."

Bert and Leo shake hands as flashbulbs pop. "Hi, kid," Leo says. "Nervous?"

"No. After where I've been, a baseball game doesn't make you nervous."

"Well, that's great, kid. Good luck to ya. And I just want you to know, we won't bunt on you tonight."

They shake hands again.

"Well, there you have it folks," the announcer says. "Leo Durocher says he is not going to take advantage of Shepard's wooden leg. That's the kind of sportsmanship that makes baseball America's national game."

Leo nods and smiles for the cameras as he walks away. Bert spits. "So Leonard's gonna 'take it easy' on me?" he spits again.

Public address: "Ladies and gentlemen... we want to pay special honor tonight... to the brave men... who have given so much... to the war effort... Please direct your attention... to the stands behind home plate... and welcome... the men from the amputee ward... at Walter Reed Army hospital."

A big round of applause. The veterans, their wheelchairs folded in front of the grandstand, wave to the fans.

The announcer continues:

"It is also... our great honor tonight... to have with us... fresh from his victory... on the battlefields of Germany... General of the Army... **Omar Bradley**!" Another roar from the crowd. Bradley strides to the pitching mound, waving to the crowd.

"And now... to receive the Airman's Medal... the Washington Senators' own... Bert Shepard!" Another roar.

Bert jerks his head up. He hadn't been told about this. He marches to the mound to stand at attention while Bradley pins the medal on his uniform to another ovation. Bert salutes, then all turn to centerfield, where the flag is flying, and the band strikes up the National Anthem.

Bert takes his warm-up throws. The first batter, Durocher, steps up to the plate. He pantomimes a bunt to the laughter of the crowd.

Shep kicks, and the first pitch is on the corner. A ball. In fact, the next three pitches are also balls, and Leo trots to first. The crowd buzz dies away.

Goody Rosen is next up. Another ball on the corner of the plate. Then ball two. Finally Rosen walks. Catcher **Rick Ferrell** lifts his mask and trots to the mound.

"Damn," Bert mutters. "I better get this ball over soon so we can have a ball game."

"Don't worry, kid," Rick says. "You're nipping the corners, but he just isn't giving you the strikes. You're doing fine." Rick slaps him on the butt.

Augie Galan, the third hitter, hits a grounder to Layne, who forces Rosen at second. Leo takes third. A hit, an error, or a fly ball, can score a run.

Tall **Howie Schultz** is up. Ferrell flashes two fingers for a curve, and Schultz misses it by a foot. Two outs.

Veteran **Dixie Walker** steps in to hit. Bert gives a big kick for a fastball, but the ball floats up to the plate, fooling Walker, who swings early and grounds to first. Bert runs over to take the throw, beating Walker, to the applause of the crowd.

The next hitter suddenly lays a bunt down along the first base-line behind Shep. Bert whirls, pounces on it, and throws him out.

Eddie Basinski drills a grounder inside first base for a double. Bert studies the next hitter, Mike Sandlock, and gives him a change of pace. Sandlock swings early and pops up.

Bert gets all three batters in the second. Also in the third. "How's the foot?" Bluege asks.

"Great."

"Can you pitch another inning?"

"Why not?"

In the fourth Bert gets one out, **Luis Olmo** hits a hard ground ball that bounces off first base for a two-base hit. Mustachioed **Frenchy Bordagaray** singles in one run. Basinski hits to Layne, who fumbles, letting a second run score, but Shep whiffs **Sandlock** to leave both runners on base.

The scoreboard reads 2-2 as Bert comes to bat in the last of the fourth. At the last second, he slides his hand up the bat barrel to bunt, and the ball drops down the first-base line. The first baseman comes in to field it as the pitcher runs to first to take the throw. The play is close, but the pitcher trips over the base, falls, and writhes in pain.

A **doctor** is called out, and eventually two teammates support the hurler as he hops off the field on one foot.

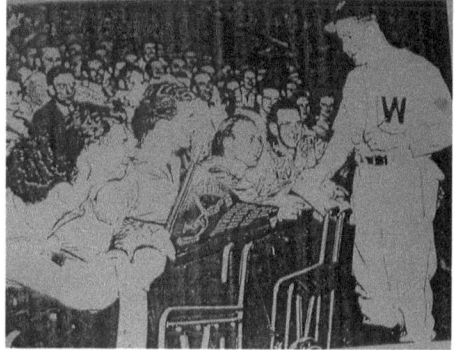

"See, Skip?" says Altrock.

"I warned you if you let Shepard play, we'd have a pitcher in the hospital."

Bingo grabs a bat and goes up to hit. He sends a long drive to the outfield. Bert streaks around second and steams into third as the Dodger center fielder heaves it in. Altrock, coaching at third, holds his hands up to signal stop, but Shep has already passed him. He keeps on running and slides into home. Safe or out? The fans are on their feet as the umpire peers at the play.

"Safe!"

A shout from the crowd.

Bert stands, dusts himself off, and jogs into the dugout past the section of war veterans, who reach out eagerly as he goes down the line, touching hands. The crowd roars anew.

"Nice game, kid," Bluege says, slapping him on the rump. His teammates give Bert some playful punches on the arm and tousle his hair.

Locker room, Shep slowly removes his leg. The skin seems raw. At the next locker, Binks winces. "Gee, why don't you take a few days off and give it a rest, Bert?"

"Heck, no," Shep pats the leg. "Nothing wrong with it. Doesn't bother me a bit. I bet I could beat you running the bases any time you say."

"The hell you could. Ten bucks says you can't."

An older man approaches on crutches, one pant leg pinned up. "Nice game, young fella," he says. He sticks out his hand. "Name's **Joe Tinker**," he says.

"Tinker?" Bert asks.

"Heh, Joe!" Altrock cries, clapping the man on the back. "This here's my old buddy," he tells Shep. "You ever heard of Tinker-to-Evers-to-Chance?"

"Sure," Bert says, shaking hands warmly. "The old Chicago Cubs double-play combination."

"Best in history," Altrock grins.

"You looked good out there tonight, kid," Joe says. "Almost as good as Three-Finger Brown. He was the best in the game back then bal. Did you know he had only three fingers? Yep, cut two of 'em off on a hay mow when he was a kid on the farm. Didn't stop him, though. Said he was a better pitcher after that. Said he could throw the curve ball better."

"Yeah, they were great players back then," Shep smiles.

"If these doctors could get me a leg like yours, I could probably go back out and play shortstop again. They keep giving me these crummy legs that don't feel right and hurt like hell."

Bert shows Joe his own leg and shows him how the ankle moves like a real ankle and the knee has the same flexibility as a real knee. "Tell your doctor to call me. I'll show him how to build you one."

For the next few weeks Bert rides the bench, waiting for his next chance to pitch.

Chick, Hollis, and the others wonder why. "Heck, we've got a shot at the pennant. You've got a good curve ball and a hell of a changeup. You could help us."

"Well, I can understand how Bluege feels," Bert says. "He's got four good starters who keep us in the ball game. Why should he take a chance on a one-legged guy in the middle of a pennant race?"

"I don't know," says Chick skeptically. "We got five double-headers coming up in five days. "I still think we could use you."

Meanwhile, Shep visits hospitals an talks to kids who have lost limbs.

At Walter Reed he visits the amputee ward. One downcast youngster, **Eddie,** refuses to be cheered up. "I ain't goin' home," he says.

"What are ya talking about?"

"I don't want anybody to see me like this. My girl friend keeps writing me, but I don't want to see her now. I'll never walk again."

"Heh! I was walking the first day. And running the second. Get up off your ass, you can do it too."

"No, I did try. I just couldn't. No strength. And it hurt too much."

"OK," Bert says. "I'll see you Saturday, two o'clock, out on the baseball field behind the gym. I'll set up a little race. If I lose, I owe you ten bucks."

Saturday. The patients, in wheelchairs and crutches, line up along the sidelines. They watch as Bert, Chick, and Hollis drive up in their Senators uniforms.

Bert: "Hollis here has got one leg half an inch shorter than the other. Show 'em, Hollis." Layne squares his hips, letting his left leg swing free off the ground. He takes a few steps with a limp. "He thinks he can beat me circling the bases. Still think so, Hollis?"

"Hell, yeah, no contest," Layne mugs, flexing his muscles.

The two men take runners' stances at home plate. "Go!"

They're neck and neck at first base. Some elbowing by both men at second. Layne runs wide as he passes the bag, Bert turns inside him and inches ahead. They bump going into third.

The on-lookers are shouting as the runners surge toward home plate. Both men slide, Shep to the left and Hollis to the right.

The dust slowly settles. "It's Shep by a splinter!" Chick announces.

"I woulda beat you," Hollis grumbles, "if I'da slid with my long leg out front."

August 5. Against the Red Sox. Bluege is almost out of pitchers. He has to use a rookie reliever to start the second game of a double-header, and he is quickly blasted for a bevy of base hits. Amid the crowd's roar, Bluege goes to the top of the dugout steps and waves a left hand to the bullpen. Shep looks to his right. Bluege shakes his head. Bert points to the left. Bluege shakes again. Shep finally points to himself.

Yes, Bluege nods. "You."

Bert hustles off the bench to warm up.

At last he is waved in. The scoreboard reads 12-1, Red Sox, with two out as he trudges to the mound past runners on second and third. Big **Catfish Metkovich,** a left-hander, is standing near the plate, swinging three bats.

Ferrell squats down, Catfish steps in, and Shepard pitches. With

two strikes and three balls, Shep reaches back and throws a high hard one, and Metkovich swings and misses.

Inning after inning Bert goes out, and after each one, Bluege asks, "How ya feeling, kid?"

"Great, Skip."

After the fifth, the guys on the bench meet him with hugs and playful wrestling.

"Three hits in five innings!" "Way to go, Babe!" etc.

Rooming house. Bingo takes a call. "Heh, Shep, it's for you. It's from **Bob Feller.**"

"Hi, Shep," Feller says. "How'd you like to play ball with Ted Williams, Stan Musial, and me?"

Bert thinks it's a put-on. "You're kidding."

"No, I'm not. I'm putting together an all-star team after the season, guys who missed a lot of years and a lot of dough in the Service. We'll go barnstorming against **Satchel Paige** and his All Stars. Coast to coast. It'll be a lot of fun, we'll split the receipts, and you'll have a little change to put in your pocket for the winter. What do you say?"

"Are you sure you're really Bob Feller?" Bert asks. "You're not pulling my leg?"

"What? And get splinters in my pitching hand? Hell, yes, I'm Bob Feller. I'll send you a confirming letter with a contract. You can check it all out. We leave as soon as the season is over."

Yankee Stadium. The All Stars take the field. Shep is introduced all around. He shakes hands with **Ted Williams,** a former Navy pilot, who asks him all about how the P-38 handles, and the two start an animated conversation with their hands.

Bert also says hi to Stan Musial, Mickey Vernon, and Warren Spahn.

He meets **Yogi Berra**. "I played you in New London when you were with the Navy," Shep says.

Paige ambles over. "You the man makes all the trees shiver with fright when you walk by?" Shep leads the laughter, all except Yogi, who doesn't get it. "I'm gonna throw you my new special pitch - the *Termite Ball*; it drills holes in all the bats."

A foghorn voice from the stands calls out, "What some guys will do to get out of the war!" Shep looks up and recognizes Tom Penn. He runs over and trades hugs and friendly punches.

A young man in army uniform waves shyly and walks over. "Hi, Son," Bert says.

"You don't remember me, do you?"

"Well..." Bert stalls.

"Eddie Kelly. Walter Reed hospital. You visited me, remember?"

"Oh, yeah." Bert glances down. "Your leg doing OK now?"

"Great!" Eddie pumps Bert's hand. "I'd like you to meet my fiancee, **Margie**."

Shep gives Margie a big hug. "You've got a good man there."

Shep trots over to first base to take infield practice. He dances around the bag, ranging to his right to cut off grounders and to his left to snare foul balls.

He takes the mound to pitch batting practice, goes into his windup, kicks his leg high - and his right foot goes sailing over his shoulder,

end over end, and lands near second base. Bert comes down on the stump and calmly follows through.

The fans and players are all in shock.

The left fielder picks up the foot like a football safety and does a beautiful job of broken field running, dodging imaginary tacklers as he runs it back to the mound, laughing uncontrollably.

Bert impatiently calls for the dumb-founded catcher, Berra, to throw the ball back. He pumps and pitches again, landing on the stump. By now everyone is laughing as Shep winds up for another pitch. He's laughing so hard himself that he can't go on and runs into the dugout - clump, step, clump, step, clump, step.

All the players rush to gather around. "Jeez," says **Yogi** solicitously. "When did that happen?"

"It was like this when I played you last year, Yogi."

"Yeah? No crap! Holy jeez!"

"Heh, get a medic over here fast," someone calls, and the team trainer pushes through the crowd of players.

After a while Bert emerges from the dugout, his foot strapped back on. The crowd applauds, and Bert lifts his cap.

"The doc did a good job," he tells the other guys. "But he worked on it for five minutes before he found out it was wooden."

Vienna airport. A Lufthansa Airliner comes in for a landing. A welcoming party with flowers moves forward as it comes to a stop. The door opens. Shep, now 70, and June emerge, wave to the applauding group at the foot of the steps, and start down. He stumbles slightly but makes a quick recovery. Grasping her waist, he makes it to the bottom..

A white-haired man steps up, hand outstretched. "Well," he says, "I see June got you across the pisser this time without crashing."

"Tom! You old. . .!" - a jet's roar drowns out the words as they hug and trade playful punches.

They all ride to a home in the suburbs, where Doctor Loidel and his family are waiting in the backyard beneath strings of colored lights. Everyone claps as the men embrace, crying a bit, and excitedly begin talking in German and English. Loidel introduces Bert to **Ingrid,** one of his old nurses, now white-haired and grandmotherly. More hugs and tears.

The doctor demonstrates how he got a hammerlock on Bert and yanked him out of the cockpit while Bert lolls his head to one side and pretends to be knocked out cold. Everyone applauds.

The group hushes and gives way to reveal a bald man standing diffidently and smiling. Bert squints but can't recognize him. The stranger says softly, "Hi, Yank."

Bert's chin quivers.

"Errey!?"

Don nods. Bert spreads his arms,

The guests crowd around. Women of all ages gush over Bert, who pulls up his pant leg to show his new, modern leg. "Not as good as yours, Don," he laughs, "but not too bad."

Boys and girls crowd around to touch the leg.

Doctor Loidel introduces Bert to his wife. **Ursula**. She smiles and coyly poses to show off her dress. She whispers to an interpreter, who asks Bert, "Guess where she got it."

He shrugs.

"Its your old parachute! You couldn't get silk dresses during the war."

An *oom-pah* band starts up a lively polka, and Bert whirls June a bit unsteadily around. Ingrid cuts in for her turn. When she sits down panting and laughing, Bert grabs an eight year-old girl for a spin while they all clap in time.

When the final note sounds with a flourish, Bert takes a little hop into the air and clicks his heels.

EPILOGUE

Still an avid golfer at 80, Burt won several tournaments for amputees. He never used a cart and walked all 36 holes on a leg he designed for himself.

MARGARET AND JOE

1950. A DEMAGOGUE BESTRIDES THE LAND. EVEN IN THE U.S. SENATE, MEMBERS ARE AFRAID TO MEET GUESTS IN THE DINING ROOM FOR FEAR OF BEING BRANDED A "COMMUNIST SYMPATHIZER." LIBERAL HUBERT HUMPHREY CONFIDES HIS CONCERN TO FRESHMAN MARGARET CHASE SMITH, THE ONLY WOMAN IN THE CHAMBER.

"WHY DON'T YOU SAY SOMETHING?" SHE ASKS.

"I CAN'T!" HE REPLIES IN ALARM. "IT WOULD BE POLITICAL SUICIDE."

"SOMEONE SHOULD *DO* SOMETHING," SMITH TELLS HER AIDE AND HOUSEMATE, FORMER COLONEL BILL LEWIS. "WHOEVER SHOULD DO IT?"

"WHY NOT *YOU*, MARGARET?" HE REPLIES.

REDS MARCH INTO PEKING
PRAGUE FALLS TO COMMUNISTS
ROSENBERGS SEND ATOM SECRETS TO RUSSIA
MOSCOW EXPLODES ITS FIRST A-BOMB
TOP STATE DEPT AIDE ACCUSED AS SPY

1950. A demagogue bestrides the land. Even in the U.S. Senate, members are afraid to meet guests in the dining room for fear of being branded a "Communist sympathizer." Liberal **Hubert Humphrey** confides his concern to freshman Margaret Chase Smith, the only woman in the chamber.

"Why don't you say something?" she asks.

"I can't!" he replies in alarm. "It would be political suicide."

"Someone should *do* something," Smith tells her aide and housemate, former Colonel Bill Lewis. "Whoever should do it?"

"Why not *you*, Margaret?" he replies.

A high school basketball player in bloomers and long dark hair in a small town in Maine, Maggie Chase is an 18-year old telephone operator, whose duty includes giving the correct time to callers. The town's top politician, **William Smith**, 39, has apparently lost his watch, because he keeps

calling. In 2018 he would have been in a heap of trouble, but they are married 14 years later.

Elected to Congress in 1936, Smith whisks her to Washington. There, though a Republican, she and feisty **"Battling Mary" Norton** wear out shoe leather lobbying for FDR's minimum wage bill (25 cents an hour, $10 a week).

When Smith dies, she runs for his seat, then for the Senate. "Ow-ah Mah-gret," as Down Easters call her, votes for America's first peace-time military draft, which passes by a single vote. She tours military bases in the South Pacific and co-sponsors a Womens' Rights amendment. She considers running for vice-president.

Meantime America is roiled by "The Red Scare." The hysteria is whipped up by demagogues, led Senator Joe McCarthy. He finds Reds and their "fellow travelers" everywhere. It could be him… It could be her…

It could be *you*.

Even U.S. Senators are afraid to invite guests to the Senate dining room for fear of being smeared as consorting with "pinkos."

In the Senate, where he has immunity from slander laws, McCarthy waves a sheaf of papers.

> "I hold in my hand a list of (indistinct) names that are known to the Secretary of State as being members of the Communist party that are still working and shaping policy in the State Department."

In the seat in front of his, Senator Smith turns. "Let me have a look at those, Joe," she says.

"Why do you want to see them?" he says, stuffing them into his brief case and snapping it shut.

When no one else will act, and **Lewis** asks, "Why not you?" she is stunned. A freshman and the only woman in the Senate just didn't do such things!

"You did all those other things," he says. "That took courage."

Smith gives in, and they agree to go to Maine for a weekend to draft a statement in strictest secrecy.

They line up Independent Senator **Wayne Morse** and five freshmen co-sponsors and run off copies at night on a Senate mimeograph.

Finally, Smith is ready to deliver her "Declaration of Conscience." She pins a rose to her blouse. "You better come with me," she tells Bill. "I don't know if I'll have enough courage."

They board the little subway car to the Capitol, and who should swing into the seat opposite but McCarthy himself. "You look awful serious, Margaret," he says.

"Well, I *am*, Joe," she says. "I'm gonna make a speech, and you're not gonna like it."

"Remember," he warns, referring to her vice-presidential bid, "I control the Wisconsin delegates to the convention."

In the Senate, Bill Knowland, the Republican leader, is droning on about foreign policy. Other Senators huddle, talking strategy or chatting, as she takes her seat. McCarthy slips into his desk behind her.

Finally, Smith is recognized. The paper shakes in her hand as she begins:

> Mr President, I would like to speak briefly and simply about a serious national condition. . . . a feeling of fear that could result in the end of everything we Americans hold dear.

One by one the chatting stops; the men turn to listen. One comes over to hear better. McCarthy scowls or holds his head in his hands.

The Democratic administration has greatly lost the confidence of the American people by its complacency to the threat of communism and the leak of vital secrets to Russia. There are enough proved cases to make this point without diluting our criticism with unproved charges.

I don't want to see the Republican Party ride to political victory on the Four Horsemen of Calumny, Fear, Bigotry, and Smear.

I don't believe the American people will uphold any political party that puts political exploitation above national interest. . . .

It is high time that we remember that the Constitution speaks of trial by jury, instead of trial by accusation. Those of us who shout the loudest about Americanism are those who ignore some of the basic principles of Americanism -

The right to hold unpopular beliefs,

The right to protest,

The right of independent thought.

The American people are sick and tired of being afraid to speak their minds, of seeing innocent people smeared.

She sits down amid silence. Another senator comes over and asks to add his name to her declaration.

McCarthy stands and silently walks out.

President **Truman** seems to ridicule her. Majority leader **Lyndon Johnson** tells Democrats to ignore the speech: "This is a Republican fight; let them fight it out." **Jack Kennedy** dodges the issue.

The <u>Saturday Evening Post</u> calls her "bone-headed... the soft underbelly of the Republican party."

But financial wizard Bernard Baruch says, "If she were a man, she'd be the next President."

Pressure is put on her speech co-sponsors, and one-by-one, except for Morse, they drop out.

A notice is slipped under her office door at midnight, saying she has been removed from her committee assignment and replaced by **Richard Nixon.**

She is given the lowest assignment, the committee on elections.

"They may regret it, Margaret," Lewis says. McCarthy publishes a doctored photo showing U.S. Communist party chief **Earle Browder** seeming to give advice too Senator **Millard Tydings** She leads the fight to expose it.

Republican leader Robert Taft scoffs that such things would not be unusual in Ohio.

"Oh?" Smith snaps. "Maybe we should investigate Ohio too!"

Dwight Eisenhower is nominated for president and names Nixon as veep. He dodges calls to criticize McCarthy.

McCarthy puts up his own candidate against Smith in Maine, but "ow-a Mah-gret" beats him, 623 precincts to three.

The men take courage: If she can safely defy Joe, so can they. The Senate censures McCarthy, who dies an alcoholic.

Smith runs for president.

CAPTAIN COMBAT

IS THIS THE GREATEST SOLDIER IN AMERICAN HISTORY?

THEN WHY ISN'T HE WEARING THE MEDAL OF HONOR?

THE TRUE STORY OF CHARLIE BUSSEY

In World War I Sergeant Alvin York single-handedly killed or captured 133 German soldiers.

In World War II Lieutenant Audie Murphy was credited with killing "about 50" enemy soldiers in one engagement. Private Jose Lopez killed more than 100 with his machine gun at the Bulge.

In Korea, Lt Charles M Bussey and three enlisted men stopped an attack of North Korean troops, threatening to cut off a U.S. battalion. The bodies of 258 enemy are left on the field.

A quonset hut, Italy. In the dark, someone shakes Charlie's bunk, but he's already awake with excitement. He heads for the latrine.

Pre-flight briefing room. They listen as the operations officer points to map coordinates and gives them rendezvous times. Then Colonel Davis strides to the front. "The Germans will fight like bees to protect their oil fields. The *ack-ack* will be as thick as a carpet, and every Messerschmidt in Romania will be in the air waiting for you. Remember: *Your job is not to get kills and glory. Your job is to protect our bombers!* That's all that counts."

On the airstrip he climbs onto the wing of his P-51 fighter with its brightly painted red tail and stretches himself to get rid of the butterflies. Above him, B-17 bombers drone toward their target. Then he climbs into his cockpit, and one by one the Red Tails roll down the runway and take off to catch up with the bombers.

In the air. The B-17s are strung out for miles ahead of him as black *ack-ack* (anti-air artillery) puffs blossom around them. One bomber is hit. Trailing smoke, it begins losing altitude. "Jump, dammit!" he mutters to himself. "Why don't they *jump*?" One chute pops open. "Where are the others?" No more chutes open. "Poor bastards." He watches the bomber spiral down and crashes. Bussey throws up into his face-mask. He lifts the mask to wipe is face with his sleeve.

Then he sees six enemy fighters coming up at a bomber from below, firing at its belly. Charlie and his wingman, Peepsight, turn toward one, guns blazing, and it explodes. Pieces of wing and fuselage fly back at them.

Charlie hasn't breathed throughout the fight. He gasps. His mouth is dry, and he wipes his cracked lips with a gloved hand.

A geisha house. 1950. Charlie, in stocking feet, is dancing the *Tanko Bushi* with several laughing *geisha*. Then he eases into a hot bath with two of the girls, who giggle and compete to soap his back.

The door slides open, and Lt **Bill Benefield** appears. "The North Koreans just invaded the South!" he says. "We're moving out at 0500 in the morning."

A railhead at dawn. Japanese girl friends and wives, with babies on their backs, wail. In one of the cars Benefield curses. "Charlie, my wife and kids are arriving from the States this afternoon."

The train pulls out.

Pusan, South Korea. A **major** meets them. "The U.S. Twenty-fourth Division is being chewed up with horrendous losses. You're all there is to hold 'em before they over-run us all and push us back to Japan. Get up to Kumchon and set up a blocking position as fast as you can."

"Kumchon?" Bussey asks. "Where's Kumchon?"

The major snaps open "The Stars and Stripes" newspaper to a map of Korea. "You're here" – he points to Pusan – "Kumchon is there."

"Okay," Charlie says. "As soon as we get all our gear loaded – he jerks his thumb at bulldozers and other heavy equipment on deck – "and get it on a train, we're out of here, sir."

"Can't help you, Lieutenant. The Korean stevedores are on strike; there's no one to unload the equipment. And no trains to load it onto."

Bussey shouts: "Benny! Chet! Sergeant Whitaker!" They hurry over. "Any of you ever driven a train?"

"Once," Whitaker says.

"Okay, find me a train and bring it here, on the double."

"Yes sir!"

"Benny . . . Chet. Can you operate these cranes?" Chet nods.

An over-weight **colonel** appears. "You can't do that! You have no authority." He drops a bedroll onto the wharf, lies down, and clutches his heart. "Call a medic!" he gasps. Charlie looks on in disgust.

In a few hours the equipment is unloaded, and the sweating men are exhausted. With loud toots of a whistle, Whitaker arrives, leaning out of a train cab, waving and shouting.

By nightfall the loaded train pulls out.

Kumchon. Battalion headquarters tent. The battalion commander orders Benefield to clear a minefield. "Sir," Bussey says, "it would be murder until the infantry clears the enemy from the hills."

"That's ok," Benny says. "I'll go."

Benefield and his men come under intense fire and topple amid the mines, which explode as they fall. Benefield is carried back almost dead, and Charlie rushes to his stretcher. He calls his company medic. "Napolean, for God's sake, <u>do</u> something!"

"I've done all I can, sir. We've got to get him to the battalion aid station."

"Well, where the hell is that?"

"I don't know, sir. They got separated back at Pusan."

Bussey curses and watches Benefield die clutching a rosary. "Goddam stupidity!" Charlie cries. "No infantry cover. No medical support. Benny should be alive now, not dead!"

Company tent. Bussey is wakened from a deep sleep to meet two new lieutenants - **Carroll LeTellier,** a blond South Carolinian with a soft southern accent, **and Paul Wells,** a white Texan. Salutes and hand shakes, and Charlie rolls over to go back to sleep, muttering, "Just what I need - two damn crackers!"

His first sergeant: "You know you just made history, sir."

"Whaddya mean?"

"I think this is the first time any white officers reported for duty under a black commanding officer."

That afternoon. Bussey gets orders to blow a crater in a road where the North Koreans will be advancing. He takes Le Tellier's platoon and a bazooka in 110-degree heat. They take up positions where the road curves around a hillside and watch the GIs march pass them in retreat. "That's all," the last one calls.

"Fire in the hole!!" Bussey hollers and twists the plunger on his "hellbox." A deafening earthquake spews boulders the size of jeeps into the air. Huge rocks rain down around them, several just missing them.

As the thick dust finally settles, Bussey stares at a great crater yawning across the road. Almost on its edge an American captain and two men lie stunned, their boots blown off their feet. Charlie dashes to them. "What the hell you trying to do, Hoss, kill us?" the officer demands.

"They told me there were no more Americans coming."

"We'll, they we're wrong. And watch out. "There's Commie tanks on our asses right behind us."

Bussey seizes a recoilless rifle - a tank killer.

The tank appears around the bend and stops at the crater lip, as though thinking what to do. Bussey raises the bazooka, aims, and fires, the backblast digs a hole in the hill behind them, just missing two men.

The round thuds into the tank, knocking off its tread. The turret turns slowly toward the Americans. Its long barrel points straight at Charlie, lying flat in his foxhole until even the buttons get in the way. A shell screams over their heads, but the tank can't depress its muzzle enough to hit them.

The Americans and the tank face each other in the heat, neither able to move. "You think it's hot out here," Charlie mutters. "How'd you like to be one of those son of a bitches in that hot box?" Gray with dust, their lips cracked with thirst, Bussey and his men wait for dark. At last, they silently slip away, and once safely out of earshot, break into a GI ditty: "I was on my way to town when *musume* (my girlfriend) called me down."

Headquarters tent. The Division commander, General Kean, congratulates Bussey - "Good work, Hot Shot" - then says, "Saddle up! The whole army is moving south, back to Pusan." He points to a map. "We've got to hold them there, or this war is over!"

Pusan. The 24th Regiment anchors the Pusan Perimeter on Korea's southeast coast.

Lieutenant Chet Lenon's platoon supports an infantry company on a patrol deep into enemy territory. That night the infantry struggles back, but no word on the engineers.

A Week later. One of Lenon's men - "Bebop" Sanders - has crawled 20 miles back to camp. Bloody, tattered, with a swollen face, he gasps that he wants see "the Man." Charlie is shaken awake and rushes to the aid station. Sanders says Lenon was abandoned by the infantry and left in a hidden valley – "I call it 'Death Valley.' They're all badly wounded and haven't eaten in six days."

Bebop points to a trail on the map beneath a high ridge. "Right about here, there's a break in the cliff – 'the Hole in the Wall.'" Bebop smiles through puffed lips. "I said no one was gonna get me before I got home to see the Yankees play again."

Bussey calls Colonel Wilson for permission to rescue his men. Wilson shakes his head: "We don't know if they're still alive. We can't risk losing any more men. Permission denied."

Charlie tells his lieutenants he's going anyway. "Sir, you're sticking your neck out, disobeying direct orders. You could be court-martialed."

Bussey calls a company formation and calls for volunteers. Every man steps forward. He picks everyone but the cooks, who protest vigorously, but he orders them to have a hot meal waiting.

"Corporal French, Private Fields, I want to see you."

"Oh-oh," Fields says, "what have I done now?"

"French," Bussey says, we'll be traveling just below a high ridge line. Any North Koreans up there can pour fire down on us. We gotta have protection up there, or we could be wiped out. I'm picking you two for the job."

French, 18, protests. "Sir, I'm just a corporal. You've got sergeants with way more experience, some of them in World War II."

"I know. But I know the kind of man I want, and I want you. Our lives depend on you two."

"Fields, when we get there, I want you to make sure nobody surprises us from above."

Before dawn, the men climb onto trucks. "If anyone wants me," Bussey tells First Sergeant Dudley, "I'm on a 'road-repair' reconnaissance." He spots the cooks in the last truck. "Heh, I thought I told you to stay here."

"Sir, we can heat up C-rations for supper. We want to go too."

"Get out of here," he orders with a chuckle, and the cooks climb down, grumbling. Then Bussey calls, "Saddle up," and swings up into the lead truck.

At the camp check-point, guards halt them. "Where you heading, sir?"

"Gonna get our goddam wounded out, that's where!"

There's a cheer from the guards. They wave his truck through.

The sun is up. The men dismount. French takes his patrol and looks up at the almost vertical 40-foot wall to the top of the ridge. "Your men will be tired in this heat, but you've got to keep them moving," Bussey says. "I don't want any surprises."

"Yes sir." The patrol begins its arduous climb.

At the top French waves an all-clear, and they begin their march. French stays several hundred yards ahead of them. A handful of North Koreans runs before him.

Finally, the track leads to a narrow 20-foot gap. The stench of decaying bodies hits them, and they find several American corpses with their hands tied behind them and their ears and noses cut off. Some men turn away and puke.

Bussey orders one platoon to take the high ground on the left, one take the ground on the right. Bussey will lead the third platoon into the valley. "Fields, you get up that cliff. If it's all clear, fire a burst. That will be the signal for us to go in. Anyone screws up, I'll have your ass. Move out!"

At the top Fields fires a burst. "Let's go!" Bussey leads them at a trot. They find three men so weak they are barely able to talk. SGT Napoleon, the company medic, hands out chocolate bars, which the men gobble without removing the wrappers.

"Chet Lenon?" Bussey calls, "Chet!"

"Over here," a weak voice answers. Charlie rushes to him. "I knew you'd come," Lenon says.

Up above, a squad of North Koreans, hearing the gunfire, trots up. "Cut loose!" Fields yells, and his squad opens up with all their weapons. The enemy are blown away or turn and run.

The wounded are put on stretchers and hastily carried out. Dog tags are collected from the dead, shallow graves are hastily dug. Bussey leads a quick prayer, and they dash back to the trucks.

At their camp they burst into "I was on my way to town when *musume* [my girlfriend] called me down " The guards cheer and wave.

Wilson arrives by jeep. "Bussey, you broke every rule in the book. You ought to be court martialed. Did you lose any men?"

"No sir."

"Did you find Lenon?"

"Right here, sir," Chet calls from his stretcher.

Wilson shakes his head. "Don't you ever do that again! Oh, I almost forgot. I thought I'd bring these over personally." He pulls out a set of captain's bars. "I'll even pin them on for you." The men erupt in cheers.

A lull in the fighting. Bussey and Le Tellier walk over the terrain. "You know," Charlie says, "This road is the only way off this mountain if the enemy breaks through. See that goat track? If we could widen it, we'd have another escape route."

A crew starts to work. The new regimental commander, Colonel Chaney, drives up. "What the hell do you think you're doing?" he demands.

"You never know when you'll need it," Bussey says.

"A waste of time," Chaney sneers. and drives away.

Bussey shakes his head to Le Tellier: "You can't win a vast war with half-vast officers."

Next Chaney orders Bussey's company to join the infantry. "I want you to protect those artillery guns back there and hold this hill at all costs!" he snaps. "And all artillery missions will be cleared through me. I'll be at division headquarters." He points to a map, showing his command post eight miles to the rear, then leaves in a cloud of dust.

Charlie calls to a GI. "Bring your B.A.R. (automatic rifle) and follow me."

The man mutters, "When I get home to Mississippi, I ain't gonna be able to vote or go to college. Why should I get my ass killed?"

Bussey overhears him: "Because if you don't get your ass moving, the damn *enemy* are gonna kill it. And if they don't, I will! And as for Mississippi, when you get home, I suggest you find a better place to live. Get going!"   Private Crowley, a chaplain's assistant, has just been assigned to the company, but he doesn't know anything about the infantry. "I'll try to straighten it out in the morning," Bussey says. 'Meanwhile, go find Sergeant Whitaker and tell him to give you an M-1 [rifle] and show you how to use it. And watch out for your boots - the North Koreans love Yankee boots."

Bussey gripes to Lenon. 'Dammit. I need engineers. But the damn army doesn't train enough colored engineers, so I get company clerks and mechanics and guys from the mess kit repair battalion."

Nightfall. The enemy attack begins with artillery fire and a screaming infantry advance. Bussey's men are firing as fast as they can. He grabs a field phone and cranks Chaney's headquarters. "Request artillery fire. sir.

"Denied. Too close to your own position."

"Colonel, I know where I need it even if it's in my own foxhole."

Chaney hangs up, muttering, "You have to know how to handle these *nigras*."

Bussey slams the phone down, then whirls and fires at a charging North Korean, who is about to jump into his foxhole.

The moon reveals the defenders sprawled in and out of their foxholes. Crowley lies bent at the waist, a knife in his throat. His boots are gone.

Bussey gets a quick phone report from his platoon leaders. Only 98 men are left out of 200. He cranks the phone and demands to speak to Colonel Chaney. "He's gone to bed, sir," a voice answers.

"Well, damn it, wake him up!"

"I'm sorry, sir, I have direct orders not to disturb him."

A rifle butt cracks Charlie in the back of the head, and he blacks out for a few seconds. He gradually focuses again, shakes his head, grabs an entrenching shovel [mini shovel], and swings it, catching his attacker in the cheek. Blood spurts out.

Sun up. The men wearily sip coffee, uniforms spattered with blood, sleepless eyes hollow. Sprdic firing is heard.

Chaney drives up in a starched uniform. 'Damn it, I told you not to give up that hill!" he barks.

"If I'd had artillery support last night, we'd still be there," Bussey snaps. "But we saved every one of our artillery pieces - didn't lose a gun. But I lost a hundred men."

"We'll, get your men, and go back up and re-take that hill!"

A stray bullet strikes the ground between Chaney's feet. He jumps into his jeep and races away down the new road, veering to a stop into a farmer's septic field.

Wilson arrives in his jeep. A whistle blows shrilly, and with a yell the North Koreans charge over the hill. The Americans scramble for their weapons. 'Dammit, Hot Shot, call for some artillery!" Wilson orders.

"Yes *sir!*"

The big guns bark, blasting holes in the attackers' ranks. The charge falters. The enemy stumbles back.

"That's a dirty wound in the head," Wilson says to Bussey. "I want you on the next train to the hospital in Pusan. that's an order."

A bombed out Korean hospital. Clean sheets. A pretty nurse, Ruby, enters, her breasts straining against her starched blouse. "Roll over," she says cheerfully, "and pull down your pants."

"Why?" he grins. "What do you have in mind?"

She looks impishly around as if making sure nobody is listening. "I'm going to pump you full of penicillin," she replies, plunging in a syringe.

"Ow, not so rough," he says.

Seductively: "I can get a lot rougher."

"Don't say that if you're just joking," he warns. "I've been at the front for two months."

Smiling: "I know."

"Heh, how long does a guy have to wait before the doctor lets him be a guy again?"

"That depends whether he has a double or a single room."

She leans forward to plump his pillow. 'Do you like white wine or red?" Ruby gives him a toodle-oo with her fingers as she closes the door with her hip.

That night she returns, quietly opening the door with a wine bottle in one hand and two glasses in the other. She flicks the light off with her elbow and quietly pushes the door shut with her hip. Moonlight bathes the room as Charlie stretches his arms to her.

Morning. Whitaker enters. "I got shot in the hand," he says. "We had a hell of a fight after you left."

Charlie throws the bed sheets aside and grabs his uniform from the closet. "I'm catching the next hop back from the Air Force."

"That's AWOL, sir."

"I don't give a damn!"

He passes Ruby, who lifts her eyebrows. He gives her a shrug and a smile. "Can't help it, I gotta go." He grabs her shoulders and kisses her as several doctors and nurses turn and stare. Then he rushes out.

At the air base. A shout rings out. "Heh! Bad Boy Bussey!"

Charlie whirls to see two pilots grinning broadly at him with a bottle of whiskey. "Peepsight!" he exclaims. "Red!" They punch each other in the biceps and wrestle. They pour him a drink.

"What the hell you doin" in those combat boots, man? Don't you know a gentleman doesn't get mud on his boots?"

"Yeah, I know, and they sleep in beds. Which I haven't done in two months."

The others are wearing majors' leaves. "What's the matter with the Army, they don't promote people?"

"Hell, no. But they give us all the <u>kimchi</u> [cabbage and strong garlic] we can eat."

"How come you got all black GIs?" Peepsight asks. "Don't they know the President ordered integration two years ago? Man, the Air Force is pepper and salt now. They liked what the Red Tails did in Italy, and I think it opened the doors."

"Hell, they don't even give us credit for anything. If we take a hill, they don't say anything. If we lose a hill, they say, "Colored troops bugged out."

"You miss the old P-51s?"

"Yeah. It's a different war up there. A hell of a lot different."

"Well, here's to the old Red Tails." They clink glasses.

The mess tent. Bussey gets a standing round of applause as he enters. Everyone crowds around to shake his hand.

"Good news, sir. We just got word: MacArthur has hit the Commies in the rear at a place called Inchon. They're pulling out. We've got orders to chase 'em out of South Korea."

On the road north. Bussey and his company roll into a town. The streets are lined with kids and others waving Korean and US flags and shouting, '<u>Me Gook</u>! <u>Me Gook</u>! A boy pulls Charlie's arm until he dismounts and follows to a farmhouse. Inside, a wounded North Korean soldier lies on rags, his leg green and smelling of gangrene. "Get Napoleon," he orders.

The medic shakes his head. "This will have to come off, but I think it's too late. The nearest MASH is forty miles behind us."

The wounded man puts a finger in his mouth, begging them to shoot him. Bussey orders the others out, unholsters his .45, puts a pillow over the man's head, and pulls the trigger.

Back on the road. The weather turns cold. The men trudge, still wearing their summer shoes and light-weight jackets.

A small Korean woman is walking along under a heavy load on

her head. Bussey's jeep stops, and she and painfully lifts her burden. From her coat she fishes out a two year-old. Then she brings out a one year-old, who starts squalling. While the two Americans watch, she hobbles to a ditch and squats just out of sight. In a moment a squeal announces a third baby has just been added. The woman wraps her newborn and returns all three babies to her blouse, stoops, and begins to pick up her burden again, but Bussey takes it away. They help the protesting woman into the jeep. "Head for the aid station," he orders.

Next day Napoleon returns to report. "They made her stay overnight, but she wouldn't take a lift. Just picked everything up and started walking again."

Later. Bussey's jeep pulls up alongside the same woman. She flashes a wide smile but motions that she is fine and gives them a wave.

Night. As the men put up pup tents and dig trenches, Bussey hears a scream from a shed and dash inside, where one *GI* is wrestling with a young girl while another holds her parents away at gunpoint. Bussey pulls them away. "Aw, Captain, we were just havin' a little fun," one says. "You know how long it's been."

"How would you like to wait fifty years for your next one - in Leavenworth penitentiary? Get the hell out of here."

The couple bow thanks. A crowd gathers. The young boys approach and run their fingers over Charlie's forearms, then look to see if the black has rubbed off. Charlie pulls up his sleeves. "See, I'm black all over," he smiles.

Using sign language, the old couple invites Bussey to supper. Hosts and guest sit cross-legged at the table on the heated floor. Toasts are drunk to everyone. Number-two wife, Kwaja, about 19, steals glances at Charlie, then quickly lowers her eyes.

The GIs force down small bites of *kimchi*.

Bussey proposes a trade: a truckload of rice for 16 <u>kaesang</u>, or <u>geishas</u>, and an empty house for a day. Kim accepts. Bussey leans over to Whitaker. "I want Napoleon at the door with a gallon of penicillin. Nobody goes in without one."

Kim and his wives keep smiling and murmuring, "<u>Me Gook, Me Gook</u>."

"What the heck's that mean?" Charlie asks.

"That's mean 'Beautiful Country.'" the student says - "'America.'"

"Oh. Is <u>that</u> what it means? I thought it meant. . ."

The meal over, the guests bow thanks and start to file out. Kim motions Bussey back, pushing bashful wife number-two forward. She goes to her bedroom door, turns, and smiles.

Winter. The Americans race north, toward the Yalu River border with China, shouting, "Home for Christmas!"

Then the Chinese invade in massive numbers, and the Americans reel back in retreat, or, as the Marines put it, "attacking to the rear."

Still clad in summer boots and wrapped in blankets, the 24th soldiers limp in single file down the road as Chinese swarm over the hills on both sides. A white unit silently tramps along on the other side. Charlie tells Pinckney, "Look at that. White boys can run as fast as colored boys."

They slog across a frozen river as bugles are heard in the hills around them. Charlie's engineers push long "bangalore torpedoes" out on the ice, where they explode, breaking up the ice so the enemy can't cross.

Charlie's phone rings. "This is Colonel Corley! Who's making all that damn racket?"

"I am, sir. We're keeping the ice broken up."

"Well, cut it out, dammit. I can't get any sleep!"

In the morning, Bussey is shaken awake. "The Chinese have crossed, sir. They're on the hills."

He springs awake. "We're moving out." The bleery-eyed men stagger to their feet and resume their bitter march.

A numbing cold night. Pinckney's breath comes in clouds as he shakes Bussey awake. Charlie just snores. Pinckney shakes again. Louder snores. Another shake. A snort and a grumble. "Wake up, Captain, Colonel **Corley** wants you at his command post in ten minutes."

Cursing, Charlie slowly wakes, shivers, and pulls himself out of his sleeping bag. "This was my first sleep in three nights," he mutters.

They arrive at Corley's tent. The colonel, a much-decorated World War II veteran, is from Brooklyn, which is clear from his speech. Charlie beats his arms. "Must be thirty below zero," he chatters.

"Nah, just twenty below... Bussey, I got a big job for you." He leads Bussey to a map. "Here we are" - he hits the map with his pointer. "And here" – he slaps it again – is a Chinese ambush site. I want you to Knock it out."

"Sir, my men and I haven't slept in two nights. This is an infantry job."

Corley ignores him.

"Here" – slap – "is another ambush site. Dey're both blocking our withdrawal route for tomorrow. Knock it out too."

"This" – another slap – "is a medical clearing station. The Chinese captured it. Clear them out and take it back."

"Sir -"

Corley waves his hand. "There's no one else can do it. That's why I'm giving the job to you." He pulls the transparent overlay off the map, folds it, and hands it to Bussey.

A trail in the dark. Charlie and 40 men hunched in their coats stumble double-file. A shot cracks. The men hit the ground, and Bussey waves them to deploy left and right. Then he calls, "Fire!" and they each pump several rounds in the direction of first shot. There is no answering shot. They creep forward, stumble over three bodies, and plod on.

A mile later they glimpse a bonfire and hear laughs and see a figure dancing. They silently advance. In the firelight they see an ambulance overturned and four dead Americans sprawled around it. Bussey shoots the dancer, the others shoot the rest. Charlie can hardly keep his eyes open, but he calls Corley. "Lion One? This is Lion Six. Both ambushes knocked out."

"Good."

"How 'bout that tank support, Sir?"

Not a chance. Not in the dark. I'll send 'em at day-break. Out."

The men are sleep-walking, and the sergeants go down the line, prodding them awake.

Ahead they hear cries of wounded and dying. "Whit," Bussey whispers, "take your men around back. Don't let anyone escape. But don't shoot until you're <u>sure</u> they're Chinese." Whitaker nods and waves to his platoon to follow him.

Hospital tent. Le Tellier and his men warily enter. Bussey turns his flashlight on and finds beds overturned, medics shot, a patient in traction on the floor in excruciating pain. From all around come groans. Bussey steps outside and calls into the dark: "Nurses! Medical corpsmen! Come on back in! It's safe."

Slowly they appear out of the dark and begin to help patients back onto the beds. The engineers assist them. They start fires in gasoline drums, find the dynamo, and start it going again. They re-kindle fires in the mess tent.

Day breaks. The rumble of tanks is heard. Mess sergeant Lamont is on the lead tank. "Hot chow!" he calls. "Come and get it!" The men limp up with their canteen cups out. Other cooks jump down and carry food containers into the tent for the wounded.

Bussey calls Lion One. "All secure, Sir."

"Good job. Come on back in. Out."

Those who can, climb on the tanks and curl up.

Next night. Once more Bussey is roused from sleep. Once more he reports to Corley's tent, where the colonel is warming his hands at a fire in a gasoline drum. "What time is it?" Charlie blinks.

"Almost midnight."

"Sir, I just got to bed."

"C'mere."

They go to the map again. "Here we are... Here's the route of withdrawal... Here's the first battalion.. . . Here's the second. But I don't know where the hell the third is. I haven't heard a peep from Colonel Bair for over twenty-four hours. He has to be somewhere over . . . here, on the other side of this hill. That's your job: Find him. The Chinese could be here in twenty-four hours. This bridge" - pointing – "has been blown, so you'll have to find another way in and then lead him out."

"Sir, that's a job for the Intelligence and Recon Platoon."

This is too important, Bussey; that's why I'm giving it to you."

'Sir, this is my third straight night without sleep."

Corley scribbles a note. "Give him this. Get goin'. There's no time to lose. Take two of your best officers. If two of you go down, one will get through."

Bussey, Le Tellier, and Whitaker hunker into the night beneath a quarter moon.

"Halt!" a shout in the dark. "Password."

"I don't know the damn password," Bussey growls. "Yesterday it was 'Golden Gate.' I'm Captain Bussey from the Seventy-seventh Engineers."

"It's okay, I know you, sir."

"Who are you?"

"Fox Company, Third Battalion."

"How long you all been here?"

"Two days, sir."

"How close is the enemy?"

"We haven't seen any since we got here."

"Can you call Lion Six?"

"No, sir. Colonel Blair took all our radios."

"Why the hell did he do that?"

"I don't know, sir."

"Where is he?"

"Follow this path. His tent's about 100 meters from here."

"Thanks, son."

Blair's tent. Bussey peers inside. "Shut the damn flap," Blair orders. "We're surrounded. We've been fighting all day and night. It's been a hell of a battle!" Blair is wild-eyed.

"Sir, Captain Bussey." He salutes. "Colonel Corley sent us."

"How'd you get through the Chinese lines?" Blair yells, his voice high-pitched.

"We haven't seen anybody. Your sentry said everything's been quiet for two days."

"Quiet, hell!"

Bussey unrolls a map. "Colonel, you have to get out immediately. He gave me this note. The Chinese have broken through, and they can cut you off. He wants you to join up with the rest of the regiment at 1500 hours. The bridge you came over is blown, you'll have to follow us back."

"I told you we're surrounded!" He levels his carbine at Charlie.

"If you wait, you <u>will</u> be surrounded." Bussey and the two others turn their backs to leave. Behind them they hear Blair pull the bolt of the carbine back. Bussey's jaw muscle tightens.

"Halt!"

They don't stop.

"That's an <u>order</u>!"

They lift the tent flap and go out into the night. Bussey is livid. The three walk silently back to the sentry.

Behind them they hear orders being shouted. The battalion comes alive. Companies are formed. Truck engines are started. A captain drives up in a jeep. "I'm Able Company, Captain," he says. "We're the lead element. Which way?"

"Follow me," Bussey says. "Can you give us a ride? I can't keep my eyes open."

Corley's tent. Bussey, Whitaker, and Le Tellier enter. "Good job," Corley says. "No one else could have done it." He shakes their hands.

As they leave, Blair enters. They hear Corley shout, "I oughta court martial you!"

Spring. Company headquarters tent. Bussey asks his first sergeant, Dudley, "Where's the third platoon?"

"The colonel attached them to Love Company; they're trying to take a town up ahead, Yechon."

"Not another infantry assignment," Bussey complains. "Who's gonna build your bridges if we all get killed?"

A mailbag arrives. "Give it to me," Charlie says. He swings it over his shoulder and jumps into his jeep with a .50 calibre machine gun mounted on the hood. "Get me a .30-calibre and an ammo belt!" he shouts, then nods to his driver, Pinckney, to take off.

They drive through paddies green with grain, where white-coated farmers bend over, harvesting the blades.

The trail turns into a narrow track between paddies. Ahead of them, army trucks are stopped, blocking the track. "Where's the engineers?" Charlie demands of a **straggler**. The man points to a hill on the right.

Bussey swears and yells, "Let's go!" They jump out of the jeep and hurry up an adjoining hill. With binoculars he scans a valley of paddies to the front and sees a mass of white-coated "farmers" marching toward them. " Must be maybe two hundred fifty men. You ever see that many farmers marching in a formation?"

"No sir."

"This is too many men. If they cut the trail, there's no way out for our troops. Those poor bastards over there" – he nods to the next hill - "will be trapped."

They scramble back down. To one straggler he orders, "Grab the .30 calibre." To another he shouts: "You, take all the ammo boxes you can carry, and both of you get up this hill!" The men don't move. "Move it!" he barks. They jump and dash to the jeep. Charlie and Pinckney pick up a .50-calibre heavy machine gun. Charlie takes the gun and a box of ammo, Pinckney picks up the tripod and another box. "Follow me."

The four grunt and struggle up the slope under the hot sun. Bussey sets up the light machine gun and orders the stragglers: "When you see those guys get in to about 100 yards, go to work on them!"

Then he dashes off to set up the heavy. Pinckney feeds the belt into the gun, Bussey pulls the bolt back. He fires a burst over the heads of the column. The men dive for cover. Then "somebody started blowing a whistle. The guy out front signals, and guys begin moving up and fanning out, taking cover behind dikes in the rice paddies." They begin returning fire. The shots whine past Bussey. "Hot damn!" he growls, "This is a hell of a lot of men. How'd I get my ass into this mess?"

He waits for the enemy to get closer, then shouts, "Let 'er go!" and both gunners fire in a frenzy. Enemy bodies explode or fly backwards.

"I was scared shitless! Absolutely shitless!" Bussey mumbles, "Goddam it! Why didn't you mind your own business?

"I didn't think I was going to get out of that thing. But there was no place to run to and nothing to do except fight."

On the adjoining hill, Fields (right) hears the firing. "Heh!" he calls, "It's the old man!" He watches 15 or 16 enemy go down. Then mortar rounds begin to explode above his head, and he dives for cover.

The infantry lieutenant runs back, yelling, "Get out of here!" Everyone takes off back down the hill.

Bussey: "They saturated my hill pretty good." A round goes off behind him. The next explodes in front of him. "We're bracketed," he mutters, still firing madly. "The third round bursts over his head,  and sharp splinters draw blood from his wrist and scalp. He wipes the back of his hand on his sleeve and continues pumping away.

The other gun is hit, and the crewmen are blown several feet through the air

Meanwhile, behind the next hill, the lieutenant calls for volunteers to find where the mortars are coming from. Fields and Womack respond.

"We found them," Fields shouts. "They're so close you can hear the "whoomp" when the shells come out of the tubes. They're firing at point-blank range, straight up and straight down. And they're very, very good. They can 'walk' the mortars right down your throat If the first one misses, you better move, because the next one'll get you."

A man from L Company is hit. Womack and Fields try to help him. They call Gamble, a medic, who runs to them, but a mortar round explodes and tears him in half.

Womack is hit in the face by the shrapnel. It picks him up "like a blast of heat flying out of an oven" and sends him sailing about eight feet away. He has fragments in his leg and side, and one in his eye. The round goes in from the side of his head and comes to rest sticking out near his eye. Fields carries him to a jeep and speeds to the aid station.

Meanwhile, on Bussey's hill, "I shot and shot and shot until my gun was over-heated and stopped firing."

"Damn!" he cusses. "Now I'm really up shit's crick!" To himself: "I don't think I'm going to get out of this thing." He mumbles the words of the 23rd Psalm: "Yea, though I walk through the valley of the shadow of death, Thou wilt protect me . . ."

"By now I've got a whole bunch of enemy in close. I shot and shot and shot until my gun was over-heated and stopped firing. That's when I was in real trouble. I didn't think the .30 could do the job, but there was no other way." He and Gamble run in a crouch to the light gun. "By now I've got a whole bunch of enemy in close," He sets the gun back up, and resumes chattering furiously.

Bodies fall left and right in the paddies below. Charlie fires maniacally until the last body has fallen in the valley. His ammo almost gone, he stops and listens to the stillness. He takes a deep gulp of air and realizes that he hasn't breathed in what seems like several minutes. He gasps to get his breath back.

"It's very difficult to estimate time in a fire-fight. it must have been seven to ten minutes, but it seemed very long, because things were happening so fast."

Then he slowly stands and peers. He and Pinckey make their way, half-sliding, down the slope. The once green paddies run red with blood. Moans are heard, and a few hands are raised feebly. "There isn't a doctor within fifty miles," Bussey grunts. He take out his .45 and walks among the bodies, stopping now and then to fire a *coup de grace* "as an act of mercy."

They do a body count. "We had a total of 258 men in that bloody puddle." They are wearing rubber shoes. Some have Russian .28-caliber 'grease guns.' Others have World War II 7.62 rifles.

Back at company headquarters Fields is shouting, "You should have seen Lieutenant Bussey! I never saw anything like it."

Bussey reports to the Third battalion commander, Colonel Pierce. "Thanks for saving my bacon," Pierce says.

Sergeant Dudley motions Bussey into the command tent. "Now, tell me exactly what you saw. Was there anyone else who saw it?"

The sergeant scribbles notes, then cranks the field phone and calls the engineer battalion. "Sir? what's the procedure for writing up an officer for the Medal of Honor?"

Back home. Newspaper headlines - the Washington *Post*, *Time* magazine etc - announce the news in big headlines. Black churches are filled with people singing praises. On the floor of Congress members rise to insert the accounts into the Congressional Record.

Next day. Bussey is ordered to take a bulldozer to level an air strip. The road takes him past Yechon, and he turns off to find villagers digging graves. He orders the 'dozer operator, Spencer, to gouge out a long trench, and the villagers push the dead into it as Spencer snaps the picture. Then Spencer dozes the earth back over.

The mass grave at Yechon. S. Spencer/77th ECC.

Fields and three other men give affidavits confirming Charlie's feat. But the other three die before Army investigators can record them.

A Korean hillside. Bussey, Pinckney, Fields, and Womack stand at attention as General Kean, the Division commander, pins Purple Hearts on their chests. Kean leans over and tells Bussey: "This is a down payment on the big one, as soon as the paper work is in."

Bussey's tent. Weeks later Corley enters. Bussey dips a tin mess cup into a can on the fire and hands the coffee to the colonel, then gets a bottle of raisin jack and spikes both their cups. They clink cups and sip in silence.

Corley breaks the silence. He clears his throat. "You know, you're a damn good officer," he begins. "You're the one I can count on to do any job I throw at you." Bussey nods thanks. Corley digs into his coat pocket and brings out a case. "Congratulations."

Charlie opens the case to find the Silver Star medal, the Army's third highest decoration for bravery.

"For Yechon," Corley says.

"A Silver Star?" Bussey says slowly. "General Kean said -"

Corley cuts him off. "I know. I downgraded it."

"We buried 258 bodies. This says 'many' bodies. . ."

"Kean and Wilson are gone. I tore the paperwork up: Look, I know nobody ever did what you did. You deserve the Medal of Honor. But no Negro has won it since the Spanish-American War, and that's over fifty years ago. And no Negro officer has <u>ever</u> won it. If you were an enlisted man, or white - or dead - I'd have okay'd it right away.

"I'm sorry, Charlie, but if you won the CMH, it would be all over the newspapers. You'd be a big hero. You're an educated man. You can talk and write. Your people would follow you. And our country can afford to have Negroes in positions of power. There's no telling what would happen."

Bussey stares at him.

"Charlie, at least I'm being honest. This is the way it is."

Corley lifts his cup in salute. "But you're one hell of a soldier, Charlie. One hell of a soldier."

He stands and offers his hand, but Bussey just looks at him. Corley turns and walks out into the wind.

The mess tent. Bussey, in a new uniform, is sitting amid his officers and noncoms as Lamont plies him with biscuits, pheasant, and raisin jack.

"How's the malaria doing, sir?" Whitaker asks.

"Better, thanks," Bussey says.

"It's been a hell of an experience serving with you, Sir," Le Tellier drawls. "You're a good man, Carroll," Charlie replies. "I'm going to write your old man and tell him so. I expect to see you wearing a couple of stars some day."

He shakes hands with each of the officers and noncoms. Holding a cane, he walks a little stiffly outside, where the company is in parade formation. Pinckney waits beside the jeep to whisk him to an airfield. LeTellier steps to the head of the foremation and takes the first sergeant's report and salute.

"Men," Charlie says, "I'll always be proud to have been one of you.

You're the most decorated company in Korea. You never got much credit. But you always got the job done. You fought beside the infantry, and even in front of them.

"God bless you."

Charlie walks stiffly but unaided to the jeep as Le Tellier calls, "Present <u>Harms</u>!" Pinckney takes the driver's seat, and the jeep rolls slowly in front of the company as Charlie holds his salute. Then they head off down the road and around a bend.

EPILOGUE

From 1863 to Vietnam 25 African Americans have been awarded the Congressional Medal of Honor, the nation's highest award for valor.

None at all was awarded during World War I and II, though seven were awarded retroactively.

Only two were awarded to black soldiers in Korea. The Army has refused to rectify this injustice.

Twenty were awarded to blacks in Vietnam, including five to officers.

The US Army's official history of the Korean war does not recognize Bussey's exploit in stopping 250 enemy soldiers. First Sergeant Dudley's statements from eye-witnesses and the recommendation which he sent to battalion headquarters have never been found.

The Army refuses to believe the photograph of the mass grave or the affidavits of Fields and others.

WITCHES' BALL

CHANCES ARE THE NEW ENGLAND PATRIOTS DON'T BELIEVE IN SYBIL, THE SALEM WITCH.

THAT'S OK. ONCE UPON A TIME SYBIL DIDN'T BELIEVE IN THEM. IN FACT, NOBODY DID. UNTIL ONE HALLOWEEN NIGHT.

THEN STRANGE THINGS BEGIN TO HAPPEN.

Sybil and Louise can whomp up a love potion or help solve a murder. But never on Sunday. They save Sundays to zap power to the woebegone '76 Patriots.

And, by gosh, the team starts to win! They even start to believe in themselves.

Though quarterback Ace Hart rages about "devil worship," he soon falls for Louise, and coach Chuck Lowell tumbles for Sybil.

When gamblers learn what's going on, the girls turn off their help, and the gamblers lose a bundle. But the story leaks to the papers, and the guys accuse the girls of stealing the glory.

"OK," they reply, "you don't need us any more anyway - if you believe in the Force."

Two nights before the playoffs, thugs seize the girls and whisk them away. They send a psychic call for the boys, who arrive miraculously in the nick of time.

The game comes down to one final play.

Do _you_ believe in the Force?

Sexy, funny, suspenseful, with plenty of football action. A Witches' ball of fun.

Based of a true story.

"ALL THOSE WILD WITCHES,
THOSE MOST NOBLE LADIES."
Poet William Butler Yeats

Rosemary DeWitt (Louise Huebner on cover) Laurie Cabot Ruth Revzen

THE PATRIOTS OF '76

Steve Grogan, Quarterback Steve Nelson Linebacker

Her black hair and cape blowing in the autumn wind, **Sybil** hurries along a mist-shrouded street past Salem's Witch Museum and the House of Seven Gables. She passes a movie showing *Hocus Pocus* with lurid posters of shrieking witches in a graveyard and wrinkles her nose in disapproval.

She passes a TV store displaying a picture of a green-faced hag riding a broom. She turns and goes in. A radio in the background is playing, "It's Magic" by Doris Day. Multiple TV sets show a football game in the background before half-empty stands.

Sybil, wearing an *ankh* and a pentacle (a star inside a circle) around her neck, cheerfully calls the store owner, **Frank**. In a lilting, sultry voice, she makes a joking plea to take down the picture.

"Do I have a wart on my nose?.... Do I cackle? [Actually she is 40-ish and good-looking].... Do I have snaggle teeth? Witches go to the dentist just like everyone else, you know."

She sees a cross above his desk: "After all, they called Joan of Arc a Witch, didn't they?"

He smilingly agrees to remove the offending picture. They shake hands, then turn to watch the TV as the quarterback, Asa Hartz, goes down beneath a heap of tacklers and announcer **Howard Cosell** cries:

"Ace is down again! His fourth sack of the game."

"Thirty-five to three," Frank sighs; "same old Pats."

"Thirty-five runs!" she exclaims. "That's a lot."

Sybil smiles farewell and leaves as an **announcer** says: ". . . Meanwhile, in other news, another woman's body has been found in a ditch outside Pawtucket Rhode Island, the third young woman found murdered in the vicinity this month...."

Sybil hurries to a weather-beaten old clapboard building with a sign creaking above the door proclaiming

CROW'S HAVEN
Potions, Fortunes, Healing Herbs
Sybil Cabot, prop

She begins climbing creaky stairs.

Meanwhile, at the stadium, the fans jeer half-heartedly and file out as the New England Patriots, their uniforms torn and faces streaked, limp into their locker room.

Quarterback **Asa Hartz** slams his helmet and wearily slumps before his locker, while newsmen besiege coach **Chuck Lowell**.

"That's four losses in five games," writer **Johnny Scribo** says. "When are you going to turn the season around?"

"Soon," he sighs, "I hope we can do it soon."

They swarm toward Ace wearing a towel. "Five passes intercepted," Scribo says. "Any comment?"

"I was throwing good," he snaps. "But the line didn't give me a hell of a lot of time." He winks at a female reporter, throws the towel over his shoulder, and saunters to the shower.

In Salem Sybil enters a kitchen above the shop, where two women are humming and busily ladling steaming liquids into bottles from a cauldron boiling on the stove. **Rosemary,** Sybil's daughter, is a pretty red-headed 17 year-old in sloppy sweater and jeans. **Louise,** Sybil's friend, is an attractive woman in her 20s, whose close-fitting pants and sweater show off a stunning figure.

Brooms rest in the corners, various sizes of shillelaghs (wands?) occupy other corners, black cats arch their backs or curl up asleep, a black mastiff stretches out on the floor, herbs hang from the ceiling rafters to dry, crystals adorn a sideboard, and on the wall hangs a shield with witches' runes written on it.

Louise's brother, **Phil**, and his buddy, **Andy,** enter dejectedly, wearing Patriots caps. Phil gives the women half-hearted pecks on the cheeks, takes a paper towel and scrapes dog *doo-doo* off his shoe. "Someone left you a little present on your front stoop," he says.

"Again?" Sybil sighs. "That's the second time this week." Louise sighs and fills a pail of soap water to clean it up.

"You could save yourself a lot of problems if you wouldn't wear those clothes and called yourself something else besides Witch."

"But that's what we are," Sybil shrugs, "just like Presbyterians are Presbyterians. It's not our fault if people say we're Satanists; what do they know?"

"Phil!" Louise exclaims suddenly. "You're wearing the Witches' pentacle I gave you!" She indicates the star hanging from his neck, and gives him a kiss. "How did the Red Sox do?"

"Patriots," he corrects her wearily. "Same old story. You know, if you glass are for real, you ought to be able to prove it."

"Well, we've solved murder cases," Louise says.

"And found that little boy lost in the woods," Sybil adds.

"I mean something big," Phil says. "Like helping the Patriots win. I'll believe in you girls if the Pats win next Sunday."

They look at each other. "You've got it!" they reply together.

Sybil: "I'm going to put it up to them, and they're going to win like you've never seen."

"Okay," he smiles. "But if they don't, I'll never wear this again. Deal?

"Deal!" Louise says, reaching up to embrace him.

Sunday. Louise sits in a lotus position and puts both heels behind her neck. Then she unwinds and assumes an inverted lotus, standing on her head with legs crossed.

Fans are beginning to gather at the stadium around pickups, lawn chairs, and picnic tables, with beer kegs flowing.

In their separate apartments Sybil and Louise turn their showers on and slowly shed their clothes. They step into the showers and let the hot water caress their hair, throats, shoulders. At last, thoroughly cleansed, they reach for towels and slowly dry themselves.

Then they gather around a large pentacle painted on the bare floor boards. All are dressed in black.

Sybil chants a spell and sprinkles a circle of salt around the group.

Louise brings a candle, a match, a pencil and paper, a piece of charcoal, a writing tablet, some frankincense and myrrh, sea salt, wolf's hair, and water. She puts these inside the circle.

Rosemary lights the incense and puts a pinch of frankincense and myrrh on it to burn, releasing a fragrant aroma.

Sybil takes the paper and pencil and writes down the thought she wants to project, a victory for the Patriots. Then she lights the paper and lets the ashes burn in the dish. They hold hands, forming an "energy circle," and count down to the *alpha*, or meditational level, and begin concentrating on "energizing" the Patriot players as the referee blows his whistle for the kick-off.

That evening the Witches are hanging herbs from the ceiling to dry, humming along with a recording of "Magic Is the Moonlight" with Dean Martin.

Phil and Andy burst in the door. "Forty-eight to seventeen!" Phil whoops.

The women look puzzled.

"The score! The Pats won forty-eight-to-seventeen! Ace never played so good - four touchdowns and no interceptions! It's a miracle!"

"Here, we can catch the highlights." He goes to the TV and dials a channel.

In their locker room the Patriots are whooping it up, squirting each other with beer. Howard Cosell weaves through the noisy room, microphone in hand, saying, "... the most lop-sided victory in the history of the New England team.... Coach.... Coach Lowell!" – he shoves his mike at the coach, whose hair and cheeks are drenched with beer.

"We never expected to win like this!" Lowell exults. "Everybody on our team played outstanding football - *everybody!*"

The screen shows a play from the game. Hartz takes the ball, drops back to pass, then spotting a hole, sprints through it and goes seven yards for a touchdown as the ref raises his arms and fans jump up and down.

Cosell moves to a knot of reporters and shoulders his way through. Hartz is holding court: Scribo shouts over the others: "Did you ever expect anything like this?"

"Hell, no. We never even thought about putting that many points on the scoreboard until it happened."

Cosell: "How do you explain it?"

"I can't. All I know is, I'm really enjoying it. We've got a Super Bowl team, and we'll be playing like one for the rest of the season."

Tackle **Pat Neville** empties a bottle on Hartz' head. "I didn't walk up the ramp in pain after the game like I usually do," he shouts. "Today I floated up!"

Cosell: "Now back to the Boston *Globe*'s **Ray Fitzgerald** in the booth."

Fitzgerald: "There was an electric atmosphere in the stadium. Even the roaring crowd was electrified."

Shots of screaming fans.

"I'm speechless. How can what is happening happen? Hartz was sensational. The special teams were marvelous. The defense was a stone wall. The coaching was impeccable. Even Oakland coach John Madden couldn't figure out what happened."

Cut to the subdued Oakland clubhouse. Coach **John Madden** is looking dazed as reporters shout questions.

"... No team of mine has ever had a worse physical beating in all the years I've been the coach. We respected their offense, but we never expected anything like *this*." He walks away shaking his head and mumbling, "They shouldn't have been able to run on us like they did. They shouldn't have been able to run like that...."

Phil folds Louise in his arms. "How'd you *do* it, Sis?"

"Anyone can do it," she smiles. "A child of three can do it - with thirty years practice."

He looks puzzled.

"We just use the Force," Sybil says. "We project our psychic energy to augment the players' own natural energies. They have the ability, they just weren't playing up to it. I can't throw the ball for Ace whatever-his-name is. He does that himself. The Force can't make me into a great piano player."

"Why not?"

"Because I'm a lousy piano player."

Andy: "They play Detroit next Sunday. Can you zap Detroit too?"

"We don't zap anybody: 'Do as ye will if ye harm none.' But if it's for the good of all, we should be able to do it every time."

Later, Andy hunches over a phone. "High. . . Nick?"

"Yeah," **Nick** answers. He is wearing a vest and talks with a cigarette in his mouth.

"Andy, here.... What's the line on Detroit-New England Sunday?"

Nick consults a sheet. "Let's see. . . Detroit by six."

Andy: "OK, give me the Pats for ten thousand."

Nick reaches for a ledger and writes. "You got it."

In Louise's apartment, a phone rings. A man introduces himself as **Detective McNulty** of the Pawtucket police. Would she be willing to help them on a matter?

She listens. "Oh, yes, that poor girl who was murdered? Of course, we'll do whatever we can.... Thursday? Well, you know this is the busiest time of the year for us – Halloween is next week, and we have that program at Symphony Hall Friday. Then we have to get ready for our charity Witches' ball Saturday night.... But, yes, of course we'll come. Eleven o'clock, at your office? Yes, we'll be there."

Thursday morning a police car turns off a highway onto a narrow lane and stops. McNulty steps out and opens the door for Sybil and Louise. "Here's where the body was found," he says, "but we don't know where the murder actually occurred."

The women survey the scene. Sybil looks at a nearby tree. "Can you cut me that branch, please?" she says, pointing. He produces a pen-knife and cuts. Then he hands her a Y-shipped limb, which she grasps by the two ends with her thumbs toward her.

She circles the area. The branch bends to the right, and she follows it off to the side. Suddenly the branch dips its head, like a bird straining for water, and she has to struggle to hold it.

"Here," she says.

McNulty stoops and inspects the ground. He picks up a button, surveys it, and puts it in a plastic bag. Then a key.

"I'm seeing a car," Louise says. "An old car. Maybe red." She walks around slowly. "And a house .... a lot of tires piled up.... a dog – a big dog."

"Where?" McNulty prompts.

She concentrates hard. "I don't know...." The limb pulls her to the left. "It must be over that way," she says, pointing north.

McNulty shakes their hands. "This has been very helpful. We'll check it all out. And we thank you very much."

Friday night. The sound track plays **Doris Day** singing, "It's Magic," as crowds file into Symphony Hall and posters advertise an evening of "Trick and Treat" the music segues to "The Sorcerer's Apprentice," and "Night on Bald Mountain."

On stage the Boston Pops orchestra is playing the final bars of "Bewithed, Bothered, and Bewildered." The MC announces his honor, **Mayor Michael Mullen,** who strides on stage with a wave.

"Good evening, Trick and Treaters," he beams. "We have a special treat tonight. And here to introduce our guests of honor is Mister **Ernest K Debs,** the Boston city commissioner."

Debs walks on, wearing a Dracula costume with hair slicked back, fangs, and a black cape drawn across his jaw. A light from below throws his ominous black shadow on the stage backdrop of a haunted Transvlvanian castle in the moonlight. Shrieks and groans are heard.

"*Goot efe-nink*," he says slowly in his best Transylvanian accent. "*Ant now ve have some real Salem <u>Vitches</u> for you, heh-heh-heh.*"

He claps his hands. A bang and a puff of smoke erupts on stage, accompanied by an organ chord, and when the smoke clears, two old hags in black pointed hats appear, bending over a cauldron of dry ice fumes. Green and red lights reveal her long noses, stringy hair, and snaggle teeth.

Suddenly the figures throw off their masks and hats and stand erect with arms open and big smiles on their faces.

The mayor: "Sybil Cabot and Louise Hoover of Salem, ladies and gentlemen!"

They embrace Debs and the mayor, who kiss them on the cheeks and lead the applause.

"You can't be Witches," Mullen says, "you're too beautiful."

They toss their heads, throwing their hair back over their shoulders and smiling broadly.

"So, tell me, how can we tell a real Witch?"

"You can't,' Sybil answers. "They could be anyone" she peers into the audience – "the person sitting next your (members of the audience steal glances to left and right) or standing ahead of you in the check-out line at the grocery .... Anybody. There are about nine thousand of us around the country. Four hundred right here in the Boston area alone."

"So what do Witches do?"

Louise: "We help children with learning disabilities. We help protect the environment. We work with police to help solve crimes. We can perform marriages here in Massachusetts. We show you how to use the power of your minds to be a better violin player, or dancer, or baseball player."

"You helped the Red Sox break a slump last year, I hear."

Sybil nods. "Well, we sent them a little 'psychic vitamin' to put more *zing* in their *zap*."

"Did it work?"

"They broke a ten-game losing streak, didn't they?"

A round of applause.

"Do you think they'll ever shake off the Curse of the Bambino?"

"There is no 'curse,'" Louise laughs. "It's their own fear of losing that is holding them back. As soon as they realize that they have the Force within themselves to do whatever they will themselves to do, they will do it."

"Can you help them?"

"Of course, if they want us to."

Mullen and Debs lead another round of applause.

Sybil reaches into a black pouch. "And now, Mr Mayor, I have something for you. It's a special magic crystal." She takes it out. "Rub this every night at nine o'clock, and it will raise your romantic vitality and the romantic vitality of everyone in the city of Boston."

Enthusiastic cheering from the audience.

The Mayor: "And now, Mr Debs has a special presentation for you."

Debs reads:

A PROCLAMATION

Be it known to *eferyone* by *zese* presents that Louise Hoover and Sybil Cabot are hereby proclaimed the official Vitches of the city of Boston and are entitled to all the honors and privileges that that title bestows. In *vitness vhereof* I have hereon set my seal.
(signed)

Michael Liam Mullen, mayor
City of Boston

Debs hands it to the mayor, who hands it to Louise and Sybil. He also hands them each an "official broom" from the people of Boston. Another *bang*, another puff of smoke, another *organ chord*, and the Witches disappear.

Saturday, *Samhain*, the holiest day in the Witches' year. On a **windblown hill** under the moon, Louise, Sybil, and dozens of black-robed Witches, both men and women, stand in a large circle holding candles, surrounded by tourists and other non-Witches. They chant in unison in memory of the Salem Witches hanged on this hill and all other martyrs - Jews of Europe, Martin Luther King etc.

Then they lead a procession down the hill to the old Salem waterfront and turn in at a hotel.

A ballroom. Guests in gay costumes and masks swirl on the dance floor; others bob for apples, and Sybil and the Witches circulate among them. Four turbaned bare-chested porters enter, bearing a *palanquin*. They set it down and part the curtain. Slowly two bare legs emerge, and Cleopatra appears - it is Louise. The guests applaud.

They assemble for a picture, and a bolt of light flashes across the group. Some scream.

"Don't worry," Sybil says calmly. "Its just psychic energy. Happens all the time here."

Monday. A phone rings in Sybil's apartment. It's Scribo, who wants to know what happened Sunday. He had heard she would zap the Patriots to a victory; instead, the team lost 20-10.

Sybil: "Oh, that. We didn't do anything. I was busy with our charity Witches' ball, and besides, a certain person bet his shirt on the game. We don't do that, we don't manipulate people for bad reasons."

Will she try it as a scientific experiment next Sunday? "Sure," she says. Scribo asks if he can meet her for an interview, and she agrees.

Scribo mounts the creaky stairs to the door marked "Salem Metaphysical Center" and taps the ancient iron knocker. Sybil and Louise smile him in.

He looks around and nods to the brooms. Sybil laughs. "Oh, people are always sending them to us."

"Where's your wand?"

"There," Louise nods to a four-foot knotted shillelagh in a corner.

"That? That doesn't look like a fairy's wand to me."

"Well, if I charge it with energy, it is, Wood is an excellent catalyst to transfer energy."

He nods at the shield. "What does that say?"

Louise: "Oh, that warns visitors that this house is protected by a white light and to do no evil here."

He sniffs. "Something smells good."

Sybil indicates a bubbling pot on the stove. "Potions."

"What kind?"

"Oh, this one's a love potion," Louise says carelessly.

Johnny pricks up his ears. "What's in it?"

"Well, first there's dried rose petals –"

"– for Venus and love," Louise interjects.

Sybil: " – and mandrake root; it's been known for centuries for love and amiability, and –"

Louise: "– basil, that's for love too; you can buy it at any grocery store."

"– Jasmine," Sybil continues, "frankincense, dragon's blood from Malaya."

Louise gives the pot a stir and comes up with an old bone.

"What's that?" John asks.

"An old bone," she says.

"What's it for?"

"Nothing. It was left over from supper. I just threw it in."

"All the ingredients are approved by the United States Food and Drug Administration," Sybil notes.

Louise: "Yeah, they made us change the original formula; it was giving everyone a rash."

"Try some." Sybil extends a bottle to him.

"What do you do?" he asks dubiously. "Drink it?"

"No, of course not, silly. You wear it like a cologne."

She puts some on the back of his hand. He sniffs it and makes a face. "Here," Louise says, pouring some in her palm and rubbing it onto his throat. "But be careful. Be sure you know what you're doing. I wore some awhile back, and that evening I bumped into Engelbert Humperdinck on the street. We spent the whole evening together. A big sex symbol for all women, and *he* was attracted to *me*."

"What about a love affair for you?"

"That's not hard to do," she laughs, "I've had quite a few."

"What are in the other pots?"

"Well, let's see." Louise lifts a lid. "This one is called 'Success' -"

"- That's the one I'd recommend for a ballplayer," Sybil says.

"What about that pot?"

"This is called 'Goodness.'"

"So how do I get some?"

"Oh, we sell them downstairs in the shop. 'Love' costs twenty-five dollars a bottle, 'Success' is fifteen, and 'Goodness' is five."

"We don't sell too many of 'Goodness.'" Louise sighs.

Then they get down to business. Around the table they sift through photos of the Patriot players. Sybil says she doesn't know anything about football, but she can examine each player in her mind's eye. She stops at one picture. "This one has a bad leg," she says.

"That's Al Fresco, the running back. He hurt it three weeks ago. He's been on the bench since then."

"I'll send him some extra healing thoughts," she nods.

Louise points to a picture: "Uh-oh, here's a big problem."

"But that's Asa Hartz," John says. "He's their fair-haired boy."

"I can't help it," she says, "I see what I see. He's unhappy, thinks he should be with a better team. He's disrupting everybody. He's not very confident. Is something troubling him?"

"Yeah. The Pats signed a new quarterback, Jack Spade, a big star in college, and I think Ace is afraid that they're grooming him to take over."

"When was this Ace fellow born?"

John consults a team roster. "He'll be 26 on December 28."

"A Capricorn!" she exclaims. "Oh my god, no wonder! We'll see if we can make him a nice person. Do you think that's possible?"

Next day the Witches and Rosemary are pouring their potions into bottles and labeling them. As they work, Doris Day is singing on the radio, "Magic Is the Moonlight." The women hum along.

The phone rings. Louise picks it up: "Salem Metaphysical Chapel. The Force be with you." She listens. Then she holds a hand over the receiver. "It's Ernest Debs," she says. "He wants us to stop using 'Official Witch of the City of Boston' on our stationery.

"Well, I like that!" Sybil says. She takes the phone. "Hello, Mister Debs?"

In his office, Debs is embarrassed. "Yes, Ms Cabot. As I'm sure you know, that 'proclamation' was just a publicity gag, and -"

Sybil: " - Well, you seemed very happy to have the publicity at the time, Mister Debs."

"Well, we'll have to insist that you remove the words from your letterhead ...."

"What about the City of Boston's 'romantic vitality?' Do you want me to take that back too?"

Debts (stuttering): "What I mean is, the legislature has given us no authority to confer such a title on ...."

Louise: "What about *your* romantic vitality, Mister Debs?" she purrs. "Shall we take that back too? I notice you haven't offered to return *your* magic crystal."

"We're getting complaints from various citizens, who feel that you are evil and perform black magic and ..."

"*Mister* Debs," Sybil says sharply, "it's a good thing we're *not* evil Witches, or you'd be in a peck of trouble right now!"

He is flustered. "I didn't say that. I meant ...."

Sybil: "*Mister* Debs, we have an official proclamation signed by his honor, and we jolly well intend to keep it!"

She hangs up and the two giggle at each other.

Sunday at the Cleveland stadium, Sybil in black, Louise in street clothes, Scribo, and a bevy of photographers descend an aisle to the field. Sybil carries a two-foot piece of wood that looks like a tree limb.

They pause at the last step. "Isn't anyone going to help me?" Sybil laughs. "I came here on United Airlines, not on a broom." Al Fresco comes over and lends her a hand. Several others spring forward to help Louise.

The rest of the Patriot players stand around diffidently. Lowell watches the scene with disapproval from the back of the group.

After an awkward pause, Art Nouveau, a black wide receiver, asks, "Why do you wear black?"

"To absorb all the vibrations of the universe," Sybil says. "Priests, nuns, and rabbis wear black for the same reason. And back in the 'burning times,' nine thousand Witches were burned at the stake or hanged. It was safer to wear black so they wouldn't get caught when they went out in the woods at night to gather herbs."

"Are you a good Witch or an evil Witch?" Sonny Day asks.

Louise tosses her head with a smile. "Do I look like I'm evil?" Some of the players grin. "I don't believe you would ask a fireman if he were a good fireman or an evil fireman, would you?"

"Then what are you?" Al asks.

"We believe in the powers of the earth and heaven," Sybil answers, "kind of like Native-Americans do."

"Touch my hands," says Art, "make them sticky."

"Okay," she laughs, touching his palms with the bough.

"Get them off the field," shouts Ace. "They're making a mockery of the game!" The women and John exchange knowing looks.

"Now I'm going to give you all magic crystals," Louise says, dipping into a pouch. "Rub them at the full moon before the next game, and they will concentrate all our energy with your own."

"Don't touch them!" warns Lucky Foote, the place-kicker. "It's the devil's work!"

"It's *voodoo*," another mutters.

One player quickly thrusts his crystal back, then hesitates and accepts it. Some of the others take theirs with curious smiles and shrugs.

"If you can help us win," Art says, "I'll leave you tickets to every game."

Across the field the Cleveland players are stretching and bending, watching the scene from the corners of their eyes. The women walk across to them. "I just wanted to let you boys know we're not going to 'zap' you," Sybil says. "We're going to send the Pats positive energy, but we're not going to do anything to hurt you. Good luck, fellows."

Sybil, Louise, and John take seats behind the Pats' bench. The women concentrate hard as Ace passes to Francis, who bobbles it, juggles it, and finally captures it with one hand.

Al takes a hand-off, finds a hole off tackle, and runs for a first down.

In the stands fans ask for the women's autographs. As they turn to comply, Ace throws again, and a Browns player snatches the pass out of the air.

The women quickly resume concentrating hard. Cleveland is forced to punt, and the Pats score on Hartz' pass.

Later a flash camera suddenly blinds the Witches. Ace is tackled with a crunch, the ball squirts loose, and a Brown defenseman scoops it up and gallops for a touchdown. The fourth quarter ends with the score 7-7.

In overtime, Ace drops back to pass, finds his receivers covered and decides to run. He picks up a block by Warren Peace, angles toward the sideline, and just does make it across the goal, inches ahead of a pursuer. The ref raises his arms, the Pats leap off their bench and rush to mob Ace.

In the stands Louise and Sybil embrace each other and jump up and down. Then they slump from exhaustion. "How do you feel?" John asks.

Louise: "I haven't been so tired since I flew to Transylvania on an economy broom."

In contrast, the Pats players run past them, whooping and hollering. "Remember how we used to limp and straggle off?" Art exults. "Now my feet are hardly touching the ground. I could fly."

In the TV booth, Cosell is saying, ".... another upset by the Pats, who don't look at all like the discouraged bunch that went 3-11 last year and opened the season as if they were going to repeat. Al Fresco's leg seems back to normal, and Hartz had his ups and downs but came up with the big play when it counted. How do you explain it?" Cosell shrugs. "Maybe it's the Witch. Maybe coach Lowell has found the magic solution at last. Maybe it's coincidence.... I don't know."

At their hotel bar, the players celebrate as the Witches enter. Al and Art offer the women drinks.

Ace has had a few already. "Don't you try to take credit for this," he growls.

Sybil shakes her head. You did it," she says. "If you didn't have the skill, you couldn't have done it."

Ace knocks another one back, discovers Louise, and turns his charm on her.

Sybil spots Lowell. "Congratulations, Coach," she says. "Your boys played very well tonight. She shakes his hand. "Ooh, what a strong hand. May I see your palm?" He hesitates, but she opens his hand anyway and studies it for a moment. "Hmmm, are you married?" Still ill at ease, he shakes his head. "Well, I can see that women are strongly attracted to you."

He blushes.

"This is your energy line." She points. "All strong leaders have it." Did you know that Aristotle wrote the first book on palmistry? Much of what he said is still valid today. I'm making a collection of athletes' palm prints - Muhammad Ali, Ted Williams. I'd be very pleased if I could take your print too. May I?"

"Well, er, yeah, sure," he stammers.

"Oh, that's wonderful!" She hands him her card. "Please give me a ring when we might get together."

On a chilly November day Chuck Lowell enters the Crow's Haven with his collar turned up and his face buried in a scarf. Sybil looks up in surprise. He's embarrassed. She invites him in, but he's double-parked. "Did you cross the fingers of your left hand?" she asks.

"No, why?"

"I always do when I need a parking spot. Go out and try it."

He drives around the block, his fingers crossed. To his amazement, a car pulls out of a spot right in front of the Crow's Haven. He raises his eyebrows and shakes his head.

Inside again, Chuck tells her, "I don't believe in all this Witch stuff, but ...."

"That's Okay," she smiles, "you don't have to." She makes a bargain: She'd really like to use football as a way to show others what the powers of their own minds can do. Would he let her conduct classes in psychic awareness for all his players?

"The owners would never permit it. The fans would laugh us off the field. The newspapers would have a field day."

"We'll let Louise conduct it in regular street clothes," Sybil suggests. "We'll call it 'motivational training.' Your boys are healthy young lads. If they just had confidence, they wouldn't have to lose another game."

Lowell does some quick arithmetic in his head. "We could win a wild-card -"

"- spot in the playoffs?" she finishes for him, laughing. "See, I'm learning a little about football."

They shake hands.

The offices of the Patriots. Sybil, Louise, and Scribo are ushered into the office of team president Dennis Dugan, who shakes their hands. "Well, Ms Cabot," he says, "Chuck has told me a lot about you. I thought the Cabots talked only to God, but I see you've been talking to Lowell." He chuckles at his own joke.

"As you know, ladies, I'm a good Catholic, and I go to Mass every Sunday - twice before every game."

"Good plan," Louise says. "I think you should keep it up."

"Well, we're grateful for any ideas you may have that can help the team."

"Well, we believe we can help your players use the power of their minds to the fullest to enhance their natural physical powers."

"Yes," Dugan nods. "Ninety percent of football is fifty percent mental."

She has to think this over.

Sybil: "I've lectured at Harvard about my 'Mind Power' theory. We both teach classes at Salem Community College on the subject."

"We have a waiting list a block long," Louise adds. "We'd like to conduct classes to teach your players how to do this themselves. If every athlete did it, they could break records like you've never seen. It would change the Olympics into super Games."

"That's a pretty big prediction," Dugan says. "How can you be so sure?"

"We'd like to make it a scientific study. If it works, fine. If it's garbage, throw it out."

"There have to be two conditions," Dugan says. "First, it would have to be strictly voluntary by the players."

"Agreed."

"Second, absolutely no publicity. If the news media got wind of this, well, you know what I mean."

"Absolutely."

'Scribo, can you keep this under your hat?"

"All I want is to write a book after the season."

"Fine. Then I guess that covers everything."

Louise: "The Power won't work if you don't give something back in return," Louise says.

Dugan: "Of course. The team will be glad to share our good fortune with you. Shall we say two thousand dollars?"

Scribo: "Mister Dugan, you know that if you get into the playoffs, it will be worth millions to your team."

Dugan: "But all we have so far is two games. That's not a lot of evidence. They could be just coincidences."

Louise: "Forty-eight-to-seventeen against Oakland? Do you really think that was luck?"

Dugan: "Well, uh, what did you have in mind?"

Sybil: "If the Power doesn't work, you owe us nothing. But if you win the Super Bowl, you owe us fif -"

"Let's not haggle," Dugan interrupts magnanimously. "Let's say ten thousand, and not a penny less."

"And you'll hire us back next year."

"It's a deal."

They shake hands.

"Oh, and one more thing," Louise says.

"What's that?" Dugan asks, worried.

Sybil: "We have two rules for the players. They must refrain from meat for twenty-four hours before every game."

"And from sex for seventy-two hours."

"I don't know about that," Dugan says slowly. "I don't think a ball player can go that long without meat."

The team gathers in the clubhouse for their first session with Louise, who draws some whistles, barks, howls etc. Lowell quiets everyone and says, "Football is not just a physical game. It's up here in the mind, too. We have trainers and weight coaches to work on the physical, and Ms Hoover here is an experienced counselor, who will show us how we can strengthen the mental."

He nods to Louise, who is greeted by more whistles and animal sounds.

"Okay, guys, pay attention. Ms Hoover is here to help us win a playoff berth."

"Do you worship the devil?" Foote asks with an edge to his voice. She smiles. "We don't even believe in Satan, let alone worship him."

"So what do you believe in?"

"We follow the old Druid religion of Europe before Christianity. You've heard of Merlin in King Arthur? He was a Witch. You know where Easter eggs and the Easter bunny come from? Witches. So does the Christmas tree and mistletoe and the Yule log. The three wise men were astrologers, who followed their star. Actually, they were not called "wise men," they were called *magi* as in "magician." That doesn't sound like Satan-worship, does it?

"We help kids with heart disease, kids with learning disabilities. We promote the environment. You can think of me as an Earth Mother."

This is greeted by suggestive snickers.

The first lesson will be visualizing. The players learn to close their eyes and "play" next Sunday's game in their minds, play by play: See what they want to happen, then make it happen. Lucky looks bored. Ace grimaces but finally closes his eyes with the rest.

"Now, I want you to think of your minds as a blackboard. Anything you write there, the mind will store up. If you write, 'I never have any luck,' your mind will write it down. The more you say it, the more emphatically your mind will write it. If you say, 'I hope I don't lose,' you're thinking negatively. But if you say, 'I feel great today. My arm feels great. I'm gonna win today,' your mind will write that down instead. It will replace the old negative message with the new positive one. You can actually make your own luck.

"Any questions?"

A hand goes up. "Yes? Mister ... Foote?"

"Is it true that Witches go around nude?" There are leers from the players.

"No, and you should be glad they don't."

"Why?"

"Because there are nine thousand Witches in America, and most of them have floppy boobs and not too itty-bitty bottoms."

Snickers.

"What about you? Do you?"

Louise thinks for a moment. "Hmmm, not really. But last night I dreamed I was dancing in the nude in a multi-colored fountain."

"What does that say about your subconscious mind?"

More snickers.

"I have no idea," she smiles.

She indicates three boxes on a table. "I've brought some magic potion if anyone wants some. I've got 'Love,' 'Success,' and 'Goodness.' You can give your credit card to my assistant, Rosemary."

Louise brings out her bag of lucky crystals. "Do you all still have yours?" A few dig into their pockets. "Good. Now I want you to rub them every night at nine o'clock for victory on Sunday. Oh, by the way, it will also enhance your sexual vigor."

Several players hurry forward to get one. "Get one for me," Foote whispers to Nouveau.

The players rush to the table and elbow each other, giving their orders. When they leave, clutching their bottles, the "Love" box is empty, "Success" is half-full, but "Goodness" hasn't been touched.

Ace is more interested in Louise. He saunters up to her and brings an apple from behind his back. "Do I have to wait until nine o'clock?" he asks seductively.

In a radio studio that night, candles provide the only light, eerie music plays in the background, and Louise lets a pet beetle, Sandor, out of a bottle to crawl on the studio table as Sybil soothingly speaks to a caller.

"I have a problem..." the caller is saying.

"Wait," Sybil says, closing her eyes and concentrating.... "Who is Alfred?"

The caller pauses to think. "My grandfather's name was Alfred," he answers slowly.

Sybil smiles and listens to an unheard voice. "Maybe that's who it is." She cocks her head and listens some more. After a moment she chuckles: "He says he wishes he were alive today, he wouldn't have to wear those stiff collars."

The caller's voice goes up an octave as he stammers, "He... he did hate collars!"

Sybil is still listening. "He says you're wondering whether to quit your job?"

The caller, excited: "Yes...."

"Alfred says you will find another one you like better.... Have you tried looking in Quincy?"

"No, not yet."

"Well, why don't you? You may be surprised .... Oh, and who is Lucy?"

"The only Lucy I know," the caller says, dazed, was my grandmother."

"Well, she just wants to say she's here too, and she sends her love."

"Oh, my God!" the caller gasps.

"Well, aren't you happy to hear from them?"

He stammers. "Y-yes, but –"

"But what?"

His voice breaks. "I-I never thought this would happen to *me!*"

Sybil smiles and hangs up.

Louise: "We have exciting news. We want to help the Patriots - that's our football team - win a game. They haven't won very many this year, but with your help, I'm sure they can win Sunday."

Sybil: "So here's what we want you to do. The game will start at eight o'clock. I want everyone to gather in front of your TVs. Then I want you to form circles and each person light a candle and send the boys a white light of positive energy."

Louise: "We have six hundred Witches here in Salem, so if everyone helps, I'm sure the boys will play their best. Will you do that?"

Just then Sandor crawls off the edge of the table. "Oh-oh," Sybil cries. "Get him, Louise, he's down there somewhere."

Louise ducks and begins searching through the hem of Sybil's robe. Sybil suddenly stands, knocking a candle out of its holder. A paper catches fire. "Get some water, quick!"

Louise clutches Sandor as smoke begins swirling in the studio. Both women begin calling at once: "Where's the ....?"

"It should be around here somewhere ....!"

Louise beats at the flames with one hand as the smoke thickens. Sybil pulls the fire extinguisher off the wall and aims it. Foam gushes over the mike, their clothes, the table. A stream hits Louise in the face, covering her hair. They scream and wave their arms wildly as smoke engulfs the studio. We hear the sound of falling objects and Sybil sputtering, "Oh!... Ouch! Sandor? Sandor? Is he Okay? ...." They both begin gasping and coughing loudly.

Before the game. The Pats' locker room. Loud rock music comes from a radio. The guys are half-dressed as tight end Francis Russell carefully builds a small pile of stones in front of his locker. "What are you doing?" the others ask.

"*Kahuna*," he says.

"Not that Hawaiian crap?"

"I don't care what you think," Russell says. "I grew up there. This is serious stuff. It's not like this is a big joke. It really works. Like, if I can get this energy flowing, something might happen."

He raises his voice. "Can we have a little quiet in here, please?" Someone snaps the radio off.

He begins chanting in a low voice and spreading flower petals over the stones. He takes a cup and sprinkles water onto them. He finishes his chant, slowly stands up, reaches into his locker, and begins pulling on his jersey.

Fans file into the stadium. A Boston *Globe* headline says

R.I. POLICE STILL
BAFFLED BY SLAYING

Another:

Lowell Asks Fans
to Light Candles

The lights go out. Tiny candle flames begin to appear until the whole stands are lit.

In the broadcast booth, Cosell is saying, " ...Those amazing Pats will have their work cut out for them tonight. First, they're up against the Jets, the best defensive team in football. Second, they have to stop the great Joe Namath, the game's number-one passer, who has completed sixty percent of his passes. Both clubs have identical records. The winner will stay in the race for the playoff. The other will be eliminated ...."

In the game Ace passes, then grabs his arm in pain. Lowell rushes Spade onto the field. Jack throws a bullet pass to Francis, who snags it just inside the foul line, but his momentum carries him into the bench. He totters to his feet with blood covering his face. He reaches for his nose, but it is on his cheek. Against his protests, medics push him onto a stretcher and carry him off the field.

Lowell looks down the bench and jerks a thumb at Sonny Day, who looks to left and right, finally pointing to himself in surprise: "Who, me?" Lowell nods, and Day sprints onto the field, buckling his helmet as he runs.

Cosell: "What's this? Number forty-three, Sonny Day? He's the second-string center!" He holds his ear-piece and listens. "He's never played a minute at end in his life!"

Spade passes to Day, who strains upward, but the ball is going to be over his head. As he desperately leaps and stretches, the ball suddenly seems to stop in mid-air and slows down as though waiting for Day to reach it. He bats it with one hand, it bounces to the other, and finally he grabs it and stumbles over the goal.

The players on the bench swarm over him as he comes off the field, tousling his hair and punching his arms. "That's the first touchdown I've made since high school!" he exults between gulps of Gator Ade. "In fact, it's the first *pass* I've ever caught since high school!"

Sam Birmingham, the team's best defensive back, makes a great tackle to prevent an almost sure touchdown, but he is hit in the face by a knee. He too is carried off the field. His replacement, Pete Moss, a cast-off from a last-place team, makes three interceptions, a club record, one of them for a touchdown.

SPADE TRUMPS ACE
Monday's headline reads.

"How do you explain all those subs coming through?" Scribo asks Sybil by phone.

"We're sending energy to the whole team, not to any one player," she replies. "They all pick up on it."

Louise sits in the bleachers as the team scrimmages. Ace overthrows a couple of passes. King takes over and throws some bullets at his receivers' stomachs. As they trot off the field, Ace, hobbling a little, detours to where Louise sits.

That night Louise is cuddling on Ace's lap. Her book, "Never Strike a Happy Medium," lies on a table beside the bed. They kiss. "You better see a dentist," she says. "I don't like the right side of your mouth."

"I just had a check-up."

"I'd go see him again anyway .... And beware of an accident tonight."

"Accident?"

"Yes, around midnight. Better be careful .... Also, is your sister Beverly having marital troubles?"

"Beverly? How'd you know her name is Beverly?"

"I don't know, I just said Beverly. I don't know how I knew ...."

She reaches for a small gift-wrapped box. "I brought you a little present."

He unwraps it to find a bottle. "What is it?" he asks.

"Oh, just a little basil leaf, a little bee pollen for go-energy - oh, and a dash of cedars of Lebanon for good health. I mixed it myself under the full moon."

He sniffs it. "Ugh, it smells."

"But it will fix up your arm," she smiles. "Rub it on like cologne and see if I'm right."

He embraces her, and she kisses him back. But as his hand seeks her breast, she breaks away. "Uh-uh, remember the rule."

"What rule?"

"You know what rule. The seventy-two-hour rule."

Ace is tooling home in his sports car when another car runs a red light. He stomps on the brakes and wrenches the wheel, missing the car by inches. The car clock says 11:57.

Louise's phone rings. "It's me," Ace purrs. "Just wanted you to know you were wrong."

"Wrong?" she says sleepily.

"Yeah, about the accident. He missed me."

"Go get your car fixed."

"But it wasn't touched."

"Go have it fixed," she says, hanging up.

Next morning at breakfast Ace bites into a biscuit and spits out a broken tooth.

He walks to his car in the apartment garage and stops and stares. It has a big gash in the fender, where someone has banged into it during the night.

A coffee shop in Kansas City. Louise is seated as Ace walks in and kisses her. "How'd you sleep?" she teases.

"Awful. How about you?"

She drops her eyes. "So did I."

"I still don't like your arm," she says. "It doesn't seem right. Did you use my little present?"

He stutters in confusion.

"You better not play tonight."

"I've got to."

"I don't think you should without protection."

Louise sits in the grandstand as the teams run their pre-game drills. Ace's throws wobble. She looks up at the lights, and two banks of lights abruptly go out. Ace gulps.

While the game is held up, he steals into the locker room and takes Louise's bottle from his locker. He enters a stall and slathers the lotion on his arm. He tries to leave undetected, but runs into Al and Warren Peace, who give him whistles and calls of "Whew, man! You smell that?"

"I think it must be *Eau de Dead Cat*."

"No, I think it's *Essence* of Mule Shit.'"

The lights flare on again, and the game begins. Ace connects on a long pass to the five-yard line, then carries the ball over on a quarterback sneak.

The Pats win, 21-14.

In the locker room Lowell beams at reporters: "I knew we could play this kind of football all along. I knew this team was better than we looked in September."

Next Sunday the Pats and Eagles take the field under a steady rain. The Pats fumble the opening kickoff. Ace can't get a grip on the ball, and a tackler knocks it loose. The Eagles recover.

At home Sybil watches and fidgets. "I never thought I'd care about football so much," she tells Rosemary. An Eagle runner breaks clear and outruns the Pats' defenders. Sybil lifts her arm and points a finger imperiously at the screen. The runner stumbles, dropping the ball. The Pats pounce on it.

"Mother!" scolds Rosemary. "I thought you said you never manipulate. And you never *zap* the other team."

Sybil is contrite. She nods sheepishly and puts her hands firmly under the seat cushions.

The next evening in Louise's bedroom, Louise and Ace are making pillow talk as the radio plays music. She strokes his arm with her fingernail and runs it down into his palm. "Oh-oh, what's this? I see a lot of love affairs here. How do you have any energy for football?" She wags her finger. "And all that drinking. You really don't need that. It's not your arm you're worried about, is it? It's Jack King."

He tries to change the subject. "Why the hell don't they play some decent music, like Sinatra?" he complains.

"You're worried that you're growing old. You think you can't compete with the young kids. It's not here" - she kisses his bicep - "it's here" - she kisses his forehead.

He's getting irritated. "Don't give me that *mumbo-jumbo*. It's not magic, it's this" - he makes a muscle. "This is what wins games."

"I know that," Louise says. "I can't throw a football. You have to do that. And you're good at it. Maybe I can help a little by making sure that things don't go wrong, so you have a chance to throw. You know, anything you want, you just have to ask. If you want it hard enough, you can have anything."

In a bedroom purr he replies, "Well, I want you," and starts to embrace her.

The song ends, and the announcer breaks in. "And now, by request, for all you lovers out there, here's 'That Old Black Magic' by Ol' Blue Eyes, Frank Sinatra."

Ace snaps his head forward, staring at the radio, then at Louise. She just shrugs, raises her eyebrows, smiles coquettishly, purses her lips, and wraps her arms around him as Frankie croons,

"That old black magic has me in its spell,

"That old black magic that you weave so well ...."

Meanwhile, Lowell is in Cabot's apartment. "Your boys are doing very good, Chuck," she congratulates him.

"I admit it. It's a small miracle."

She arches her brow. "Small?"

"Okay, okay, it's a hell of a - a heck of a - miracle. I don't know how to explain it. I'm a good Episcopalian. I go to church every Sunday. You know how I feel about you, Sybil. But I just can't believe in your Witchcraft."

"Well, don't, then," she says gently. "Think of it as your own fears and doubts that were holding you back."

"What about the injuries?" he asks. "We haven't had a bad injury in weeks."

"Good teams don't get injuries," she replies. "Bad ones do. The bad playing causes the injuries, not the other way around. When businessmen face troubles with their business, they sometimes get heart attacks. It's a form of excuse: 'Don't blame me; if I didn't get this heart attack, I could have saved the business.' The Pats don't need excuses now, so they don't need injuries. In fact, they don't need me any more either."

"What?! You can't let me down now, just when we have a shot at the playoff."

"Well, I have other important things to do. I've got my classes to teach. And I promised that nice Detective McNulty in Pawtucket I'd go down there and try to help him with his murder case...."

"But, we only have to win the last two games to get in the playoff!"

"All right. Just once more. Honestly, I never thought I'd care so much for a bunch of big dummies." She stands on tip-toes to reach his lips. He kisses her passionately.

Sunday morning Sybil, Louise, and Rosemary look through the Crow's Haven's ancient glass windows, streaked with rain. "What'll we *do*?" Louise frets. "You know the Pats are no good in the rain. We have to make it stop, Sybil, I know we can. We broke that heat wave last summer when all the air conditioners were going out in old folks' homes."

"But I promised we wouldn't interfere. What if we just send the Pats energy to make the ball sticky?"

"Wouldn't that be unfair to the other team, Mom?" Rosemary asks.

Sybil nods and shrugs. "Okay, get your brooms. We've got work to do."

At the old Salem wharf, the three women are hunched over, black hoods pulled over their heads against the rain. They dip their wands in the water, drawing interlocking circles on the surface. In a trance, they chant an incantation. The raindrops on the water slacken and slowly stop. The clouds scud swiftly away. A feeble ray breaks through.

At the stadium, the raindrops no longer bounce off the puddles on the Astroturf. Fans furl their umbrellas. The ground crew squeegees the water into the drains. The players doff their slickers to limber up.

Cosell exclaims, "The weatherman seems to have been wrong this time, folks. It looks like that Nor'easter he promised is going to miss us, after all."

Ace, Al, Art, Warren all play inspired ball. The Patriots win.

Sybil, Louise, and Rosie leap to their feet in front of the TV and hug.

In the locker room Chuck talks to the players. "Great game, Ace. Two touchdowns, two hundred yards passing. You really beat the devil out of them"

Sybil and Louise exchange looks and roll their eyes.

"Would you say this was one of your best games in your career?" Cosell asks Ace.

He nods. "Yeah. Everything clicked. The pass protection was great. The receivers all got in the open. My arm felt terrific. When you play like this, you can beat anybody in the world."

Cosell: "You guys were one-and-four at the beginning of the season. "Since then you've won six straight. The papers are calling you the Miracle Pats. Is it true you have Witches helping you? What about that?"

"Witches didn't do this," he snaps. "*We* did it."

Lucky butts in. "They're Satanists. I don't believe in that *voodoo* crap. They're trying to hog all the glory for something we did."

"How about that, Coach Lowell?" Cosell asks.

"Well, the boys did a terrific job. They never gave up. Even when things looked awful, they kept fighting. I knew we could do it."

"You've got to win next Sunday against the Raiders, who have a perfect record except for that one game they lost to you, forty-eight-to-seventeen. How do you explain that?"

"Well, like I said, we finally played up to our potential. And ten percent more. I told the guys if we just started to believe in ourselves, we could accomplish miracles, and we did."

"So it wasn't Witches?"

Chuck smiles and shakes his head.

Cosell: "They say the Raiders have gone to Kenya and brought back their own witch doctor for the game. Any comment?"

Ace: "Witch doctors don't scare us. We've got to beat them on the field, and we know we can do it."

Sybil snaps off the set. "Well, I like that! Satanists, huh? Little do they know." She mimics Chuck: "Witch doctors don't scare *us*."

Louise mimics Ace in a cocky masculine voice: "Witches didn't do this. *We* did."

Rosie: "Those dummies haven't learned anything you've been trying to teach them."

"Well! I'm not Mary Poppins. I don't *have* to help anyone. Let's see how they can do without us."

Monday evening Ace is knocking on Louise's door. "I'm not home," she says through the door.

"Come on, baby," he says in his best bedroom voice. "You know I need you."

"No you don't. You don't need anyone. You're full of yourself."

The door remains shut.

Chuck calls Sybil. "I'm sorry, I didn't realize how it would sound. I know I shouldn't have said those things."

"Well, I think it's time you were on your own, anyway. You were right: It wasn't us. The Force is in you if you believe hard enough. I wish you good luck, Chuck. I mean that. I'll always care for you."

"I'll send you passes to the game," he says. "I hope you'll be there."

"We'll see," she says. "I have to go to Rhode Island. I promised Detective McNulty."

"That serial killer? I don't want you getting involved. Stay out of that, promise me?"

"We'll see."

The Raiders call a press conference. Their witch doctor, Doctor Agunga, wearing a business suit, is introduced and bows self-consciously.  His grandfather and great-great grandfather were witch doctors on the shores of Lake Victoria, he explains. He specializes in helping childless couples and predicting political races; he says he correctly predicted the death of President Kennedy, the fall of the Berlin Wall, and the victory of Nelson Mandela in South Africa. He also helps a soccer team, the Simbas, in Nairobi, where every team has a witch doctor.

"How did the Simbas do?"

"They won the all-African championship last year," Agunga replies modestly.

Agunga is shown a photo of the Pats, plus a Pats jersey and helmet. He plucks a small *marimba* with a thimble, goes into a trance, and waves a tassel made of a lion's tail over the artifacts. Then he sprinkles a powder ground from a buffalo's horn and announces the score will be nine-to-seven.

Sybil and Rosie watch on TV. "Between you, me, and the wand over there, I think this guy can do it," Sybil says. "We'll just throw up a protective screen to neutralize it."

She hums to herself as she sprinkles sea salt in a circle on the floor.

The phone rings. Sybil answers. "Salem Metaphysical Chapel. The Force be with you."

On the other end, a voice says, "Hello? Mizz Cabot? This is Sergeant O'Malley from the Pawtucket police...."

Sybil: ... . Yes, sir, whenever you say... We'll be there."

She hangs up. "He wants us to go down there tomorrow morning."

On the practice field, Foote is kicking field goals, when he winces and begins limping. Lowell rushes over, and the trainer supports Lucky off the field.

A bar. Ace picks up a girl and is drinking and boasting loudly. She pulls him outside and half pushes him toward her car. She starts to get into the driver's seat, but he pushes her aside and slides in under the wheel, screeches out of the parking lot and into the fender of a passing car.

HARTZ NABBED FOR DRUNK DRIVING

On TV Cosell reports, "Asa Hartz has been freed on the team's recognizance. He was unhurt, and team officials say he'll be physically able to play Sunday. But how will it affect him psychologically as he faces the biggest game of his career? And if he can't do it, will the brilliant but untested rookie, Jack King, be ready to take over?"

Ace calls Louise and begs her to forgive him. He'll do anything to make things right again.

"This is something you have to face yourself," she says. "No one can do it for you. I gotta go now. We're due in Rhode Island in an hour. Bye, dear. Good luck Sunday."

"I love you, Louise."

"I love you too, Ace."

Louise and Sybil drive down the Interstate past a sign to Pawtucket. They hit the brakes, pull over, and back up. They pull off the highway and drive past a dilapidated house and suddenly look at each other. Louise does a 360. "Do you feel what I feel?"

Sybil nods.

They turn into the driveway and slowly approach. An old red Ford in need of paint sits out front. A mountain of tires is piled behind the house. A dog strains on a chain, barking.

From an upper window the camera watches the two women get out and cautiously head toward the house. Sybil takes Louise's hand

and squeezes reassuringly. "We are bathed in a rose-colored light of security," she says, and they both repeat, "We are bathed in a ...."

They mount the creaking porch steps and stop, unsure what to do. From around the side of the house, a man appears. Louise whispers, "I think we better get Mister McNult...." as a hand covers her mouth from behind. Sybil whirls and her arm is roughly bent back behind her.

In the Pats' locker room after practice, Lowell circulates among the players. He stops at the training table, where a trainer is taping the kicker's injured foot.

Lowell moves on, biting his lip.

Meanwhile, Sybil and Louise are trussed up in kitchen chairs in the waning light. Through the window they can see the man, in boots and a hunting jacket, chopping wood, his rifle propped against a stump. "Call McNulty," Sybil says, closing her eyes and concentrating hard.

"And Ace," Louise says, closing her eyes too.

In the locker room, the players dress into their civvies. "Get your car," Lowell says to Hartz; "I'm worried."

"Me too," Ace nods.

They head for the parking lot, their steps getting faster until they jump in the car.

"Where to?"

"Rhode Island."

"Then what?"

"I don't know."

The tires squeal as they roar off.

At the old house, the man clumps into the kitchen and slowly sits at the table opposite Sybil and Louise, who sit silently, tied to kitchen chairs with their eyes closed in deep concentration. He raises a whiskey bottle and takes a swig. The sunlight grows dimmer.

Ace's car approaches the Pawtucket exit. Chuck jerks his head. The car swerves across two lanes of traffic and screeches up the exit ramp.

In the kitchen the man takes a knife from a drawer. Outside the dog puts his head on his paws and whimpers. The man turns back toward the women when the door flies open.

Two figures hurtle into the room and tackle him. They wrestle. Chuck is thrown to the floor. Ace swings.

The man raises his knife. Sybil hops her chair over and gives him a push from behind with her heel. The knife clatters to the floor. Ace aims a punch and misses, falling off balance. The man grabs the whiskey bottle, smashes it on the table, and advances toward Chuck, who is on his knees. As he passes Louise, a sharp kick to the groin doubles him over. A hard uppercut from Ace, and the struggle is over.

Outside, a flashlight stabs the dark and mounts the stair. McNulty and three policemen appear. Ace and Chuck undo the ropes. Ace is breathing hard and stammering. "I can't believe it…. The car just drove itself…. I don't know how we got here."

Louise and Sybil exchange looks and smile.

Sunday afternoon the skies are dark as snow clouds scud above the field. Agunga parades in front of the Oakland bench, waving his lion's tassel. Chuck and Ace scan the grandstand, but Sybil and Louise are nowhere to be seen.

As the game begins, Jack opens at quarterback. Two passes are incomplete. He is caught behind the goal line and tries to scramble, but he is sacked.

A few flakes begin falling.

On their next possession, Lowell puts Hartz in. On a running play, Warren makes a great block as Al picks up 40 yards. Foote tries a field goal, but it veers to the right.

The Raiders begin a drive downfield. Agunga waves his tassel, and the Oakland fans clap in time to it. Oakland scores to make it 9-0 as the half ends. The teams trudge off as the snow has begun to stick to the grass. It is swirling around the players' feet when the second half opens.

Lowell looks into the stands and does a double take. Three black robes appear. Hartz sees them too, and his eyes meet Louise's. All three women wave their Patriot pennants as the kickoff whistle blows.

After a Raider runner fumbles, the Pats take over. Ace throws to Art, but a Raider wraps his arms around him, and the ball sails over his head. Art whirls around to the referee, who is looking up at the sky. "He held me! He held me!" pointing to the defender. The ref finally looks at him but says nothing. All the Pats rush over, shouting, but the ref turns his back.

The next play is another pass to Art, who is crunchingly hit with an elbow through the face mask, which knocks his nose out of joint. As he picks himself up, a Patriot hand reaches in and twists the nose back into position. "Good as new," he grunts as Art staggers and nods.

Chuck calls Sonny on the bunch. "Get in there!" be barks.

The team breaks from the huddle. Just as Ace bends to call the signals, he closes his eyes. In soft-focus slow motion he sees himself dropping back to pass ... a lineman breaks through with a lion-like roar, but Warren shoulders him away... Sonny runs a pattern to the left, then breaks suddenly right... the ball is up... Sonny stretches for it....

In the stands, the three Witches squeeze hands.

In real time the play develops exactly as he had visualized it. Sonny juggles the ball on his fingertips, finally holds it, skips past one defender, runs for the sidelines, and scores. He falls to his knees and crosses himself.

The two-minute warning sounds. The snow begins swirling more thickly as Agunga plays his *marimba* and chants. The Raiders drive to the 20, but the Pats make a magnificent effort and block the field goal.

On their possession, Ace hands off to Al, who finds no hole. On the side-line Lowell crosses his fingers. Warren opens a narrow hole, and Al scoots through for a long gain.

Louise, Sybil, and Rosie jump up and squeal.

The big clock is counting down: 16... 15... 14...

Ace finds his receivers blocked and decides to scramble and goes out of bounds on the 30.

The clock stops at two. Time for only one more play, a field goal from 48 yards.

Agunga gestures with his tassel, and the wind picks up, whipping the pennants at the top of the stands. Foote will have a strong crosswind to the right.

"Mother, *do* something!" Rosie implores.

Sybil shakes her head. "It's their game, dear. Let's see if they have the Force or not."

"*Please*, Mom!"

"Okay, get me a wand!"

They search their sleeves. Louise brings out a wooden nail file and discards it. Rosie begs the other fans for something wooden. After a hurried search of pockets, someone offers his pennant staff.

"Too skinny," Louise says. An elderly gentleman offers his cane, and eager hands pass it to her. She seizes it, points it skyward, and clicks into a trance.

One by one the flags fall limp.

The Pats' center bends over the ball. Warren steels himself on the line. Al hunches forward, protecting the kicker. Ace blows on his fingers and kneels to take the pass, his face contorted in concentration. Lucky looks dubious.

"You can *do* it, dammit!" Ace growls. "*See* the path of the ball, the ball will follow it. *Make* it happen!"

The Witches squeeze hands.

Agunga chants quietly.

The snap is wide. Ace reaches out and just snares it. The two lines collide in slow motion.

Ace puts the ball down. It slips from his fingers. He rights it.

Lucky has to skip to adjust his timing. His toe hits the ball.

It's up. Raider hands stretch high. It grazes their fingers. It's veering toward the right upright.

The Witches gasp.

Foote looks up.

Ace stares.

Chuck is motionless.

The ball smacks the pole.

Freeze frame.

A streak of lightening crackles above the stadium. A deep, sepulchral male voice is heard:

"Which way does it bounce? What do <u>you</u> think? Do <u>you</u> believe in the Force?"

As the closing credits roll, the Voice intones:

The ball no notice takes of ayes or no's,
But left or right, as strikes the player, goes.
But He who threw thee down upon the field
He knows about it all - HE knows - <u>HE</u> knows.
"The Rubayyat of Omar Khayyam"

SOLVEG'S SONG

AN UNLIKELY PAIR - ALCOHOLIC SOLVEG, 38, A VETERAN CLIMBER, AND GIMPY, POT-SMOKING EDDIE, 19, AN ARTIST AND STUDENT OF BUDDHISM - SET OFF, ARGUING, BENEATH LORDLY SNOW PEAKS.

TEASINGLY, THEY READ THE KAMA SUTRA TO EACH OTHER, AND AT A MOUNTAIN HOT SPRING, GIVE THEMSELVES UP TO LOVE BENEATH THE PEAKS.

AS THE SNOW GROWS DEEPER, THEY STEEL THEMSELVES TO CROSS THE LAST PASS. CAN THEY OUTRUN TONS OF "WHITE DEATH?"

AND IF THEY DO, CAN THEIR LOVE SURVIVE?

Benares, India. "Solveg's Song" from "*Peer Gynt*" plays as Solveg, 40, and her companion, Jean, about 30 and the prettier of the two, glide in a rowboat on the Ganges, where bathers of all ages are taking ritual baths. The camera zooms to the burning ghats on shore, where dead souls begin their journeys to Nirvana.

Next the women in pigtails and hiking clothes hand their backpacks to luggage attendants and board a two-engine plane.

Once skyborne, they point excitedly out the window to the range of white peaks in the distance. To the strains of "The Hall of the Mountain King" from *Peer Gynt*, the camera pans across the peaks until it rests on one. "Is that Everest?" Jean asks excitedly.

Solveg nods.

"Which one is Annapurna?"

Solveg points to the West. "That's it. The world's ninth highest peak.... my Shangri La."

The summit soars into the blue sky, a plume of snow blowing off it. Suddenly an avalanche begins to billow down the slope.

Next we look down on terraced rice paddies and scattered buildings, then the one-eyed dome of the Buddhist temple of Kathmandu, as the plane descends.

The lively folk song, "Ritsum Tiri-Di" ("I Dance Around and Round") plays while the women walk wide-eyed into Durbar Square of the old city, gobbling up the sights - open-air barber shops, green-grocers, donkey carts, kids running up and down temple steps.

Two handsome Americans, Nick and Phil, join them. A flirtation begins, and both guys center their attentions on

Jean. Phil asks where they're going. "To the other side of Annapurna," they say.

"Alone?" the guys ask in surprise: The avalanche season is coming, and two women can't get over by themselves.

The girls exchange winks and, with a laugh, suddenly open their jackets together, revealing T-shirts adorned with a snowy peak and the words, "A Woman's Place Is On the Top. The guys want to trade, so the girls pull theirs off and hand them over; the guys do the same, laughing.

The four climb the long steps leading up to the city's main temple, with a giant Hindu eye painted on the dome. They stop to drop coins in alms bowls of the maroon-robed monks, who murmur, *"Namaste"* with their palms together.

A western youth, Eddie, a bit on the flabby side, sketches the scene beside his own bowl, but the three ignore him.

On the way down, Jean clutches her stomach and slumps onto a step. Solveg calls for aid. Eddie,

hastens to help, moving with a slight limp, but Nick has already picked Jean up and carries her down the steps. Eddie calls a taxi in Nepali, and Jean is driven to a clinic.

In her hotel room, "Solveg's Song" is heard in the background as Solveg brushes her hair in the mirror and pulls at the wrinkle lines around her eyes. She arches her neck, pinching it to check for fat. She spots a gray hair and pulls it out, sighs, and belts back a jigger of whiskey.

The theme plays again as Solveg walks alone through the suburb of Boddhinath, watching cremation fires lick at the wrapped bodies. A foot sticks out from the flames. Other forms under covers on the ground await their turns.

She bumps into Eddie. "How's your friend?" he asks. Solveg says Jean had appendicitis and has been flown back to India. Eddie says he's sorry.

"You know what they do with the ashes?" he asks, indicating the pyres. She shakes her head. "They scatter them in the river, so they'll flow to the sea; the soul becomes a tiny drop of water mingling with all the other souls in the great World Soul."

Solveg listens but is annoyed by his attention. Eddie, however, won't go away. Walking back toward town past a kaleidoscope of vendors and shops, he dogs her steps and persists in asking questions.

He introduces himself.

"Hi, I'm Solveg," she says.

"Solveg?"

"Yeah. Norwegian. I'm from Minnesota."

"There are no mountains there."

"Tell me about it."

"So what are you doing in Nepal?"

She and Jean had planned to trek to Pisang monastery, Solveg says a little testily.

"Looking for Shangri La, huh?"

"Sort of."

"Paradise. . ." Eddie says. "I saw it on the late night movie once - what was the name?"

"*Lost Horizon*."

"Yeah. This guy's plane crashes in the Himalayas, and he finds this hidden valley beyond the pass, where everything is perfect, all the women are beautiful, and nobody ever gets old."

"Something like that."

"So the trip is off?"

She bristles. "I've climbed more mountains than you've ever seen - the Matterhorn, the Andes."

"But you can't travel alone, it's too dangerous. The men here don't know what to make of western women anyway." He indicates some Nepalese teenagers ogling her over their sun-glasses.

"Don't worry about me," she says. "I've got a guide."

"Let me go with you," he suddenly says. "I've lived here six months and I always wanted to make a trek. I can speak the language. I'll be good, I promise."

Solveg looks him up and down. "How old are you?"

Eddie draws himself up. "Nineteen."

"You sure?"

He squares his shoulders and repeats it. Well, he admits under her gaze, "going on" 19. With a shake of her head, Solveg excuses herself and walks ahead alone.

Later, in Durbar square (more "Ritsu Tiri-Die") Solveg strolls with her Sherpa guide, Lakpa, among the shops and temples. He is dimpled, tousle-headed, with an impish, boyish grin; his short pants show off powerful legs. They watch kids play jump rope, pass vendors hawking their wares, and barbers giving open-air haircuts, and weave in an out among the strolling shoppers and bicycles.

Solveg stops at a stall displaying a red cross and begins an earnest conversation with the shop keeper as Lakpa stands helplessly by with an embarrassed grin. Just then Eddie passes and stops. "Want a little help?" he asks Solveg.

She considers, then says, "Yes. What's the word for 'tampon?'"

Edie speaks to the shop-keeper, who nods and comes back with a pair of crampons, for climbing on ice.

Solveg throws him an impatient look. "Not crampon. *Tampon.*"

Eddie gulps, thinks for a minute, then beckons the shop keeper closer and whispers, blushing, his face pinched in thought as he struggles with the language. The woman looks quizzical. He tries again as a small crowd begins to form, enjoying the show. Again she shrugs. A young girl suddenly sees the light and blurts out a word in

Nepali. The crowd laughs, and the shopkeeper beckons Solveg into the shop.

She emerges a moment later clutching a package. She permits Eddie to walk alongside them.

"Why do you want to go to Pisang?" he asks.

"Because a very good friend is buried near there. She and I climbed Acongagua in Argentina together. You know what that is?" He shakes his head. "It's the highest peak in the western hemisphere. Then she was on the first American team to climb Annapurna and was killed in an avalanche. I've been planning to come here ever since."

"Gee, that's too bad. They all got killed, huh?"

"No, two women made it to the top .... So what brings *you* to Nepal?"

Eddie gives a half-laugh. "To get away from my father." And to study Buddhist art. His mother sends him monthly checks.

"What does your father say?"

Eddie shakes his head. "They had a big fight about it."

"So what do you do here?"

"Sketch. Smoke a little *hashish*."

"You'd never make it over the mountains," she says, poking the flab around his belt. Lakpa grins. "It's over two hundred miles, a three-week hike, round-trip. The trail goes around Annapurna. It will soon be winter, and I have to cross Thorung La pass. That's almost eighteen thousand feet. Do you know how high that is? It's almost a mile higher than anything in the forty-eight states. Pisang is on the other side. I've already lost precious days, and I don't have any time to lose. I've got to cross Thorung La before blizzards or avalanches close it.'

"Let me go," he begs.

She scoffs. "Look at you. You're not in shape. I'll have to cover ten or more miles a day, five miles up and five miles down. You'll slow me down."

Lakpa points to his own waist and shakes his head at Eddie.

"No, I won't," Eddie protests.

"What's the limp?"

"I popped my knee playing football. No big deal. I can walk okay, I just can't play ball."

"There are no doctors on the trail," Solveg says. "If you get sick or injured, I can't help you get back. When Maurice Herzog first climbed Annapurna, he lost half his fingers and toes. Altitude sickness can give you splitting headaches, cause cramps. The only treatment is to come back down immediately. I'm not going to give up my trek to rescue you."

"I promise, you won't have to."

"No," she says firmly. "This is not your trip. This is *my* trip."

"I can help."

"Don't worry about me. It looks to me like you ought to worry about yourself." She turns her back on him and walks away.

On a crisp sunny morning Solveg and Lakpa stride out on the trail. He carries her gear. She wears earphones and a tape recorder, and we hear Beethoven's Sixth Symphony, the "Patorale." With a stave in hand, she turns her face toward the mountains, passing villagers and shops. It's harvest time. Farmers thresh grain with oxen, and women winnow it with staves. A roadside blacksmith hammers a sickle. Old women turn spinning wheels. A housewife squats to wash dishes with mud. Boys play hoops and marbles. Girls carry brothers or sisters on their backs; others play on homemade swings or shyly offer marigolds. Little bare-bottom ones squat in the road to relieve themselves. A sick old man lies on a pallet beside the road. Two younger men lift it to their shoulders and go off on a rhythmic pace toward Kathmandu.

"Boddhinath," a woman nods.

Above them and around them, the magnificent mountains embrace them. A bend in the trail reveals a breath-taking snowcap rearing above yellow paddies. "The Hall of the Mountain King" from "Peer Gynt" swells on the soundtrack.

Beneath a peepul tree Solveg drops her day pack, leans against an ancient stone bench, takes swigs from her canteen, and tries to converse with a group of porters who have also stopped to rest. They smile broadly and reply with sign language and chatter she doesn't understand; they all exchange bows and *namaste*'s.

The sun has dropped behind the mountains, and a sign on a stone hut says "Hotel." Solveg and Lakpa spread their blanket rolls on bare wooden dormitory beds. She massages her feet, then goes to the "dining" room for a supper of rice and lentils. She orders some *rakshi*, native rum, and takes a belt. They meet a group of French youths - girls in pigtails and guys in beards - returning from Thorung La. One couple in their sixties is from Switzerland. A lively conversation proceeds in French and English, plus broken Nepali for the pretty hostel keeper. The travelers have come over the pass. They say they haven't met any trekkers going the other way for a day - too close to avalanche season, they shrug.

Suddenly, the door opens, and a new traveler stumbles in from the dark. It's Eddie. Solveg throws him a cross look as he limps over to the table and un-shoulders his pack. He forces a smile through his fatigue as if to shrug, "See, you didn't think I could make it, did you?"

Next morning, under a bright morning sun, Solveg, in an ankle-length sarong, sets out with Lakpa, followed by Eddie. She tells him to go back, but he follows a few steps behind. To Dvorak's "Moldau" the trail follows the sparkling river far below.

At the next rest stop, Eddie slumps down on the trail to rub his feet. Solveg and Lakpa picnic on a lunch prepared by the hotel. She is entertaining kids, showing them Poloraid pictures of themselves and letting them look through the zoom lens of her other camera.

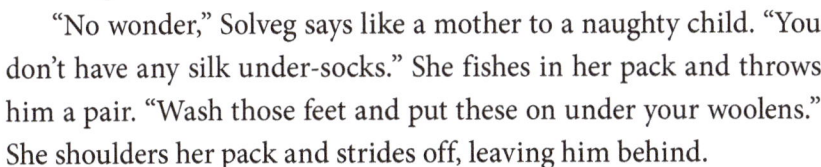

Eddie limps up. "You're crazy," she snaps. "I told you I can't let you slow me down. I'm sorry, but I've got my own plans. I'm not a baby-sitter."

Eddie has removed his boot, revealing bloodstained socks. "Blisters," he winces.

"No wonder," Solveg says like a mother to a naughty child. "You don't have any silk under-socks." She fishes in her pack and throws him a pair. "Wash those feet and put these on under your woolens." She shoulders her pack and strides off, leaving him behind.

Eddie rolls a reefer, lights up, and watches them go.

As the sun goes down, he has caught up again and trudges silently beside her. They come to a stream with rocks for footing to cross. Solveg starts over, slips, and plops in the water. Eddie and Lakpa splash to her. She pushes them away, but the more she tries to get up, the wetter she gets. Eddie can't help laughing, while she unleashes a stream of angry words. Finally, she lets Lakpa take her pack and accepts Eddie's hand with a scowl, and they slosh to the other bank and squish up the trail toward the next lodge.

She finally smiles and puts out a hand. "Thanks."

"*Namaste*," he replies, putting his palms together. "There is no word in Nepali for thank you."

"Oh? Well, *namaste*, then,' she replies with the hand gesture.

"You can't even say, 'You're welcome,'" Eddie says. "They don't say that either."

"What do they say?"

He laughs. "They just say <u>namaste</u> for everything. It's kind of like <u>aloha</u> or <u>shalom</u>. It means anything you want it to: 'God be with you.'"

"But what if someone does something nice for you?"

He shrugs. "They accept both acts of kindness and acts of meanness without comment. And apparently without judgment."

She presses her palms together and nods a silent *namaste*.

"How do you know so much?" Solveg asks.

"I haven't just been laying around smoking pot," he laughs. "I pick up things."

On the trail the next day Eddie dashes into a ditch and begins pulling up grass. "What in the world....?" Solveg wonders, raising her brows.

"Marijuana," he cries, stuffing several handfuls into his pack.

At the next rest stop, Solveg suddenly exclaims, "My camera! I must have left it back up the trail." Lakpa cheerfully doffs his pack and runs nimbly back up the stone steps in the hillside. A few minutes later he returns with the camera, hardly out of breath. She thanks him profusely.

They resume their trek, Solveg and Lakpa in the lead, Eddie striving not to fall too far behind.

The path is steeper now. Ancient steps lead upwards out of sight. Showing off, Eddie bounds ahead, taking them two at a time. Solveg and Lakpa climb steadily on. Rounding a corner in the trail, they pass Eddie, who is sitting, wrists on knees, wheezing. Without a word, Solveg plods past him. "Wait," he calls between gasps. She takes a few more steps, finally stops, and turns.

Eddie is rubbing his knee. "Ouch," he winces. "The damn thing popped out again." He sits and rubs it.

"Is it going to be all right?" Solveg asks.

"Yeah, this happens every so often, but it doesn't last."

"No more football for you, huh?"

"Hell, I don't care. My father played for USC. My brother plays for USC. I was supposed to play for USC, but I really didn't want to. My old man never forgave me."

"That's the reason you left home?"

"One of 'em."

He stands and tests the leg with a few steps. It's a little tender but seems all right.

"You'll never get there like that," Solveg says. "You've got to pace yourself like mountain climbers do." She demonstrates, taking slow, careful steps, breathing deeply as she goes: "In on the left... Out on the right."

Sheepishly, he emulates her. Solveg and Lakpa trudge ahead. He hears them laughing together as they turn a corner and are lost from sight.

At the top of the trail, Solveg plops to rest as Eddie catches up. "According to this map, we've just climbed twelve hundred feet in forty-five minutes."

"That's two Washington Monuments!" he exclaims. "More than one Sears Tower! If anybody told me I could do that, I'd say they were off in Shangri La somewhere."

"Well," Solveg says, "where do you *think* we are?" She's still huffing.

"I thought you climbed the Matterhorn," he teases her.

"I did. Twenty years ago. It's a little harder now."

At the next town Solveg and Lakpa skirt a huge Tibetan mastiff on a rope. It snarls and snaps viciously at them and catches the end of Solveg's skirt before she can pull it free. Waving his stick defensively, Lakpa leads her away. But with a lunge, the beast breaks loose and leaps on Solveg, who goes down, screaming and rolling to avoid the fangs.

Lakpa springs forward, flailing with his stick, which snaps in half across the dog's back. With a bark, the dog turns and pounces on his chest, knocking him backward. It goes for his leg as Lakpa desperately tries to kick its head away.

Eddie rushes up, still limping, and swings his pack at the dog, which snarls and turns against the new attacker. It jumps. He tries to push the head away with his hands, but his elbows are slowly forced to bend.

Then, suddenly the dog yelps and runs off. Solveg has whacked it with her own walking stick. Eddie is shaking, and Solveg is sobbing nervously while villagers rush up to help.

Lakpa is bleeding from a large gash in his calf and foot. Solveg and Eddie help him to a hotel.

Next morning Lakpa makes a show of walking, but he can't fake it, and it is clear that the wound is too severe to continue. Solveg pays him off, and they leave him to recuperate until he can make it back. She staggers a bit under her own now heavier pack as she and Eddie set off.

A crowd of barefoot kids besieges them crying, "*Mitai! Mitai!*"

"Candy," Eddie explains. "But no good for their teeth." "Here," he says, bringing out a balloon from his shirt pocket. He blows and twists it into a dog's shape, and gives it to one of the kids. They all clamor for one, and he blows and twists as fast as he can while Solveg watches with amusement and snaps their photos. Some of the girls hold out marigolds in exchange, and she snaps their pictures too.

A three-year old stretches her arms up to Solveg in the universal children's gesture: "Pick me up." She reaches down and takes the girl in her arm. Other kids immediately crowd around, all gesturing and calling out.   Resignedly, Solveg puts the first one down and hoists another. Finally she is hoisting two at a time.

"Heh," she calls, "doesn't this line ever get any shorter?"

"No," Eddie smiles, "birth control hasn't been a very successful program here. I wish I'd brought some postcards. They like to look at pictures of America."

Solveg puts her burdens down and fumbles in her pack. "Here, this is the Empire State Building. How do you say that in Nepali?"

The kids look at it quizzically. Eddie explains to them. "I said it was 'American *himal*' - American mountain," he laughs.

The kids all talk at once.

"They say, 'Do you have any children?" Eddie interprets.

Solveg unzips her belt pouch and produces a photo of a pretty blonde teen-ager posing beside a swimming pool with palm trees in the background. The children snatch it and study it intensely. "My daughter," Solveg says.

"Very pretty," he says. "In school?"

"No, she died. Last winter. Leukemia.... She was sixteen."

"I'm sorry," he murmurs.

The kids hand the photo back, and everyone exchanges *namaste*'s.

They trudge on. Eddie drops his pack and slumps. "I feel rotten," he mumbles. "My stomach."

"What's wrong?"

"I think... old Montezuma's got me," he moans. "I thought I was

immune... but I must have eaten something." He suddenly turns away and throws up.

She helps him off with his pack and tries to carry both, one on each shoulder.

Eddie waves her away. "You're already behind schedule...We've got a couple more hours of daylight...You go on; I'll be all right."

"Well, I can't leave you here."

He quickly fishes through his pack, brings out a roll of toilet paper, and stumbles behind a rock with it.

When he comes back, he is pale and unsteady.

"Can you make it to the next town?" Solveg nods to a distant pueblo of stone houses straggling up a hillside.

"How far is it?"

She consults her map. "About three miles."

She looks up at the sun, already getting low as shadows begin to creep up the mountainside. "Eddie, if you hold me up, and that pass is closed, I'll kill you."

"Let's go," he says weakly. He tries to pull himself up by his stick but falls back.

"Damn it, Eddie, we had an agreement!"

He nods feebly and waves her on. She turns and begins walking. After a few steps, she turns again and walks back. She reaches down for his pack.

"No." Eddie pulls it feebly back.

She pulls it out of his hands and opens it and begins pulling out his sleeping bag, heavy jacket, flashlight, and three books.

"What are you doing?"

"Lightening your pack," she says, stuffing the things into her own. He tries to protest but is too weak. Solveg brings out a book, *Nepali Made Easy*, weighing it in her hand. She finds a second one, *Buddhist Art of Tibet*, heavier than the first, and shoots him a glance.

A third tome is *Kama Sutra*. She arches her eyebrows.

"I brought everything I own." He can barely whisper.

Solveg fishes some more and brings out a box of pencils and several sketch pads. "Leave them all," Eddie says. "You can't carry everything." She ignores him and stuffs them into her pack too. One pad falls, and the wind whips the pages. It lies open on a study of her plopped in the streambed and angry. She can't help smiling and pushes it into her pack too.

Solveg holds out her hand and helps Eddie slowly to his feet. She adjusts his pack on his back, then hefts her own with a grunt, staggering a bit under the new weight. He smiles a thank you, and they slowly resume their walk.

The twilight has deepened when they reach their next lodge.

Eddie flops on his bed. Solveg brings a glass of *rakshi* [native rum] for herself and a thermos of soup for Eddie. She lifts his head and spoons it out, but he shakes his head weakly, and she gently puts his head back.

The morning finds Solveg sitting on her bunk leafing through Eddie's sketches. There are pages of children, old people, dogs, babies, mountains, shrines etc, followed by some of her eating, sleeping by the trailside, in close-up, in profile etc.

She picks up the *Kama Sutra* and browses idly. The pages turn more slowly, and she finally stops at a picture of a couple making acrobatic love. She stops flipping and reads.

The sun hits Eddie's eye, and he squints painfully. "How you feeling?" she asks.

"OK," Eddie says uncertainly. "A little better.... Well, still lousy, actually.... If I was home, I'd say I was too sick to go to class." He smiles wanly. "But what can I do? When your only job is to put one foot in front of the other... you just have to walk it off."

"You want some eggs?"

Eddie claps his hand to his mouth and almost vomits.

Solveg unfolds the trail map. "The next town is five miles away. Do you think you can make it by lunch time?"

He falls back on the bunk and lies inert. Finally he forces himself up, fumbles for his shoes, ties the laces with shaking hands, slowly shoulders his pack, and shuffles out into the sun.

After a little lunch at an inn, Eddie is better. "Eat a little," she urges.

"Damn it!" he explodes. "You're not my mother! My mother is ten thousand miles away. If I wanted a mother, I'd go back to California."

Solveg is taken aback by the attack.

"I'm sor-," Eddie begins.

"Okay," she smiles.

While they rest, a party of six Israeli women joins them, and they all fall into conversation. The women crossed the pass three days ago, and it had already begun to snow; they don't know how much longer it will stay open. They haven't passed anyone else for two days - Solveg and Eddie are the last ones going west.

Eddie is surrounded by the women when two male trekkers arrive and unlimber their packs. One nudges him: "Pretty good deal, huh? Seven girls all to yourself." "Yeah, lucky guy," the other grins. The women cock their ears.

"Oh," Eddie groans, shaking his head and heaving a sigh as if he's carrying an unbearable burden. "You don't know what hell I've been through.... I haven't slept more than an hour a night for the last week.... Look at me - I'm so weak I can hardly walk. I've lost twenty pounds.... I can't go on like this. I've got to get some help soon or it's gonna kill me."

He steals a glance at Solveg, who pretends she isn't listening and turns away to hide a smile.

The others bid them "*Ciao*" and head off down the trail.

Passing a village, Solveg and Eddie stop to watch an *al fresco* school in progress. The kids, including girls with kids on their backs, pay more attention to the visitors than the books, and finally the teacher, a young man, lets them take a break, and they shyly crowd around the Americans. Eddie asks one little girl how old she is, then repeats the question slowly for Solveg, who tries it out and gets a response in Nepali with eight raised fingers.

"What's your name?" Eddie prompts Solveg. She tries it haltingly, and the kids all chatter at once.

Eddie blows balloons, which the kids clutch at excitedly. He sketches some faces and gives them to the models. Solveg pulls out her family pictures and postcards. Then she produces a Polaroid camera, which is a huge hit as the kids watch in wide-eyed delight while the images emerge. They squeal and giggle and point to each other.

With a wave, Eddie and Solveg trudge upward. They pass a line of ponies coming the other way, the lead pony with a tassel f a long ascent, they stop to admire the view. Far below, the river winds, while across the valley Dauligiri Peak rears its icy head high above them. The faint sound of bells and children's voices wafts across on the clear air. Solveg studies her map.

"You might be a hiker yet," she says, playfully punching his gut. "Did you know you're standing on the side of the deepest canyon on the planet, from the bottom of the river to that mountain top?"

"I'll drink to that," he says, and they slip into benches at a table at the local "hotel." Bright paper flags wave on ropes from house to house. He speaks to the waitress, a pretty girl, and relays her reply. "We're in luck," he says, "a wedding." He orders in Nepali, and the waitress puts a paddle into a roadside oven and pulls out a huge chocolate cake. She cuts two large slices, and presents them, still steaming. The hungry hikers gobble them and wash them down with *rakshi*.

"Still hungry?" he smiles and says something to the girl, who pulls a steaming apple pie from the oven and cuts two more slices, which they also devour with much finger-smacking.

Eddie belches, sits back, and rolls a reefer, which he offers to Solveg. She shakes it off: "No thanks, one vice at a time is enough."

Full and happy, they follow the sound of music till they come to a farm courtyard, where dancers are performing before the bride and groom and a crowd of villagers. It's obviously a courtship dance, with many smiles, winks, and modestly averted eyes passing between the dancers to the amusement of the audience. Solveg snaps pictures while Eddie sketches, then she grabs Eddie's hand squeezes, and nods at the dancers: Both the lover and his beloved are boys.

After supper at the next lodge, they sit on a bench outside, watching the yellow harvest moon rise behind the peaks. She has a *rakshi*, he puffs on his joint.

"Your husband just lets you come to Nepal alone?" Eddie asks.

"Why should he care?" she shrugs.

"I would," Eddie says.

"He left me."

Eddie waits.

"A younger woman."

"He's crazy."

She smiles gratefully.

"Is that the reason you're going to Pisang?"

She considers for a moment. "One of them. I want to be in touch with Laurie again. I want to know about myself. Maybe find God again."

Inside, they spread their bedrolls on adjoining bunks. She hands his sketch pad and books back. "Have you read this?" she asks, nodding to the "*Kama Sutra*."

"Sure." He turns to a page with the corner turned down.

[Reading:] "When the heads of two lovers are bent towards each other, and kissing takes place, it is called a 'bent kiss'.... When one of them turns up the face of the other by holding the head and chin and then kissing, it is called 'a turned kiss'.... Lastly, when the lower lip is pressed with much force, it is called a 'pressed kiss.....'"

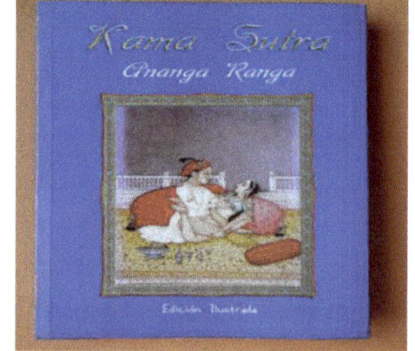

She grabs the book and reads to herself. She giggles and shakes her head. "What is it?" he demands, grabbing for it. She holds it away and they wrestle for it. Laughing, she promises to read if he won't grab:

"When one of them touches the tongue or palate of the other with his or her tongue, it is called 'the fighting of the tongues.'"

She closes it. "That's enough, young man," and the end blows out the candle.

In the morning, sunlight crawls down the opposite mountainside as "Morning" from *Peer Gynt* fills the soundtrack and Solveg and Eddie resume their hike. The wind snaps Buddhist prayer flags as they pass a *chorten,* or trailside shrine. "Each flap of the flag sends a prayer to heaven," Eddie says as they pull on heavier jackets.

They come to a wall down the middle of the path with Buddhist prayer wheels. Solveg starts to pass on the left, but he stops her. "Always pass on the left," he says, leading the way and spinning the wheels with his right hand. "Each turn is a prayer."

She sets the wheels spinning as well.

"What did you pray for?" he asks.

Solveg just shrugs and smiles. "And you?"

"To get away from my parents," Eddie laughs.

"And have you?"

He shakes his head. "Not yet."

The trail leads to the river, where a rickety bridge of rope and planks sways ominously, high above the white water. "Looks like it's time to build a new bridge," she says anxiously. He relays her comment to a party of four Nepalese farmers about to go across. They laugh and say something back in Nepali.

"They say," Eddie translates, "that they wait for the old one to fall before they build a new one."

"Well," she says warily, "this one looks like it's just about ready. I don't think it can carry six more people."

They watch the porters one by one nimbly go across the planking, one hand on the rope handrail. The bridge bounces and creaks with every step. The porters trot off on the other side.

"Ready?" Eddie smiles. "Who wants to go first?"

Solveg eyes the bridge.

"You go," Eddie says. "I think it can take at least one more."

Gingerly, Solveg mounts the bridge, carefully placing her footsteps like a tightrope walker and refusing to look down. Her boot slips off a plank, but she recovers, takes a deep breath, and goes slowly on. At last she is on the other side.

Now it's Eddie's turn. He too slides one foot ahead of the other, listening to the river breaking against the rocks below. A rotten plank snaps, and the two halves drop into the snarling whitecaps, leaving a narrower foothold in front of him. "I'm going try to jump over," he calls nervously. "Can you get my pack?"

Solveg swallows hard to and gingerly starts back across the bridge. The weight of two bodies makes the bridge sag dangerously. She drops to her hands and knees and edges toward the gaping hole. Then she rises on her knees. He carefully hands his pack across to her, leaning out over the hole. She grabs the pack, almost lets it slip, but pulls it in. Then she carefully begins backing up on her knees, pulling the pack with her. He retreats to the other side to take weight off the bridge. At last her feet touch the earth, and she rolls off to solid ground.

Now Eddie starts back across. While Solveg watches with her heart in her mouth, he slowly stands unsteadily, gets to the hole, looks down at the raging river, and freezes.

Solveg is praying silently: "You've got to do it," she whispers, "you've got to do it."

Eddie makes a move to jump, but loses heart. He tries again but can't go through with it. Finally, clenching his fist around the rope, he leaps but slips on the wet plank on the other side, and one foot goes over the side.

Solveg emits a cry.

Desperately, Eddie grasps the rope with both hands as his other foot also goes over. He sways in the air, his feet kicking wildly, seeking solid footing.

Solveg gasps and mounts the bridge again. Moving more quickly this time, she grabs his waist. With all her strength, she pulls. Slowly, very slowly, he gets his torso back onto the plank. She strains and pulls again. One knee is on the bridge. Then the other. Still terrified, Solveg cautiously begins to back away to take weight off the bridge.

Now it's Eddie's turn. He crawls painstakingly bit by bit to safety, where they both collapse, sobbing nervously and shaking, in each other's arms. She draws into a fetal position and buries her head in his chest. They lie together, panting heavily, too frightened to speak.

At last Eddie mumbles softly. "*Ki.*"

She looks inquiringly.

"*Ki*.... Soul force.... Nepalese holy men have it.... They can do great deeds... like split a board with one hand like *karate*, or knock a man down with one finger." He looks at her. "But I never saw anybody really use *ki* until you did." She hugs him, and he holds her against himself.

After supper, their nerves are calmer. They enjoy their *rakshi* and *hashish* on a bench outside the inn, watching the moonrise.

"Can people really do all those things?" Solveg asks.

"What things?"

"You know, like the pictures in the book...."

"Yeah, but it takes a lot of practice."

"They must break their backs," she laughs.

"Not if you do it in water. It's easier then."

"How do *you* know so much?"

He shrugs. "That's what the book says."

Later, a moonbeam lights part of the wall as the "Moonlight Sonata" plays and they lie on adjoining bunks. Solveg whispers. "You awake?"

Eddie rolls over toward her.

"Would you do something for me?"

He props his head on his hand, all ears.

"Would you rub my back?"

He reaches a hand inside her jacket.

"How about 'pressing with the nails?'"

"What's that?"

He quotes from memory: "When a person touches the chin, the breasts, the lower lip, or the *jaghana*, . . ."

"The *what*?"

". . . . the tummy - so softly that no scratch or mark is left, but only the hair on the body becomes erect from the touch."

"Wait a minute." She wiggles around inside her bag, rearranging her clothes: "Here." She has pulled her shirt up, exposing her back to him, and he slowly strokes until she drops off to sleep.

The next morning they walk out into the sunlight to the strains of Grieg's "Morning" and stop in awe. A snowy summit rears above the valley.

"Annapurna!" she gasps. "Isn't it *beautifuall!*"

"You know what Annapurna means?" Eddie asks. "It means 'Bountiful Woman.'"

"I don't like the ring of that," Solveg shudders. "Sounds like she's harvesting people. Eleven people have gone up and never come back, did you know that?" He shakes his head. "And I don't want to be one of them. We have to get over that pass before the storms begin."

They pass herders with yaks. Eddie points out a Nepalese eagle soaring against the deep blue sky. Sheep graze on the mountainside. "Blue sheep?" Solveg wonders.

"If they are, we're lucky," Eddie says. "Almost no one has ever seen one."

Tibetan traders sit cross-legged on blankets beside the trail, offering souvenirs for sale. Eddie picks up a metal Buddha and turns it over. It says,"Made in Hong Kong." "These people have probably been to more places around the world than you or me. They fly everywhere to buy souvenirs to bring back and sell to us."

They eat lunch bantering with kids, who swarm around. Eddie goes to his pack and fetches a frisbee and scales it to them. They scramble to catch it, then throw it back. The game of toss goes on amid squeals from the kids until a rumbling noise makes them stop.

The "Storm Movement" from Beethoven's Sixth plays, as across the valley an avalanche billows down the slopes of Annapurna. A cloud of crystals boils up from the hurtling snow. While Solveg and Eddie watch, snow begins to fall on them. "Look," Solveg says, "the avalanche has created its own weather. It's making snow fall even here. I've seen this in Chile."

"Wow," Eddie says, watching the display across the valley in wonder. "You ever get caught in one?"

"Yeah, once," she says.

"What's it like?" Do you have any warning?"

"You can't hear it. Suddenly everything gets quiet. That's how you know."

"What do you do?"

"Try to run - if you can. When you're up to your knees in snow, that's not easy."

"So what do you do?"

"Try to get behind some shelter."

"Yeah, but what if you can't?"

"Well, then you try to "swim" to the top. If you get covered, stick one hand up as high as you can and hope someone will see you. The other hand, hold over your face so you'll have some breathing space."

"That's it?"

"No. You also pray."

Night comes on, catching them on the trail. Mussorgsky's "Night on Bald Mountain" creeps onto the sound track, and they realize they are lost. They try several directions, but can't be sure. "Look!" Eddie says, pointing up the trail. "What's that?"

"Where?" They both squint into the half-dark and can just make out a form in the distance.

"Yes!" Solveg says. "It's moving." She gets out her binoculars. "My God!" she gasps. "It looks like a bear. I don't know...."

"There aren't any bears here." Eddie takes the glasses. "I don't know *what* it is. It's on two legs, and it's heading off that way."

"I never saw anything like it," Solveg says. "Let's follow it."

"Are you kidding? You're crazy!"

"Come on, it won't hurt us. It's too far away."

"Yeah, but we're already lost. Let's not make it worse."

"Whatever it is, it knows where it's going, and we don't. Come on."

Solveg starts off. Eddie reluctantly follows.

At last moonlight reveals a building. "Thank God, there's a lodge!" Solveg cries, and they rush toward it.

Inside, Eddie asks the inning-keeper about the mysterious beast.

He nods and says something in Nepali. "He says we probably saw 'The Old Man,'" Eddie says.

"'The Old Man'"?

"Yeah, that's what they call him. He lives on that mountain, and sometimes he steals dogs and chickens."

"Well, whatever it was, it showed us the way."

Two other couples, Road and Dolly from Australia, and Ichiro ("call me Itchy") and Keiko from Japan, are already eating.

After supper they all sit outside to admire the moon. Rod brings six shot glasses on a tray and passes them around. "*Rakshi*," he smiles. "Damn good." He demonstrates by taking a few sips. He offers the tray to Solveg, but she smiles and shakes her head.

New snow had already begun falling on Thorung La when they came over the pass, the other couples say. They're not sure how much longer it will be passable.

Rod takes out a harmonica and begins softly playing "Waltzing Matilda." Dolly sings the lyrics, and the others hum or sing along. A Nepalese joins in with a one-stringed lyre, another brings out a small squeeze box, a third thumps a small drum on his lap, and they play the rollicking "Ritsum-Tiri-Di." Nepalese women and children squat around to watch and clap. Rod picks up the beat, and the Nepalese men choose partners with the other men, surprising everyone with their steps. One invites Eddie, and when they split, he gets Solveg up to waltz. They split and invite Itchy and Keiko. The Nepalese women giggle and refuse Eddie's invitation to get up. At the end of the chorus, the dancers collapse, laughing.

"Where in the world did they learn that step?" Dolly laughs.

Eddie asks them. "In the Kathmandu disco," he translates.

The Nepalese beg another song. Itchy sings a Japanese folk song, "*Tsuki ga*" ("The Moon Comes Up"), switching to English lyrics after one verse:

"Mr Moon slowly rises,

"O'er the mountain he rises, *yoi-yoi*..."

Rod joins in on the harmonica, and the Nepalese musicians also pick up the tune. Keiko interprets the lyrics (a coal miner watches the moon rise from inside the deep shaft of his mine), and Eddie translates for the Nepalese. Keiko dances a pantomime, geisha-style, (digging coal etc) and motions everyone to form a conga line behind her and follow her steps. On the edge of the firelight, even some Nepalese women and kids pluck up courage to mimic them.

They all beg Solveg and Eddie for a song next. She begins to hum some bars of "When the Moon Comes Over the Mountain" ... "Moonlight in Vermont" ... "Moon River" ("wider than a mile"), and "By the Light of the Silvery Moon" (I want to spoon).

Eddie breaks in with "On Top of Old Smoky" (all covered with snow) -

Solveg repeats the refrain:

"I lost my true lover

"For courtin' too slow...."

Eddie looks at Solveg, who drops her eyes. The echoes fade over the fast-darkening valley. They sit watching the sky, the stars, and the mountain shapes against the dark.

One by one the other couples stand, stretch, and retire. Solveg and Eddie sit, unwilling to break the enchantment.

"What are you thinking?" she asks.

"Just wondering. Are you a woman from the Ganges and the Jumna Rivers? Or a woman of the Audhra country?"

"What's the difference?"

Once more the *Kama Sutra* comes out of his jacket pocket. He thumbs to a page and reads: "The women from the Ganges and Jumna are noble in their character, not accustomed to disgraceful practices, and dislike pressing the nails or biting."

"Oh? And the other?"

"The women of Audhra have tender bodies and have a liking for voluptuous pleasures." He smiles at her sidelong. "They are full of passion and make slowly the sound of [he imitates] 'suh suh.'"

"It doesn't say that," she laughs and tries to grab the book, which he holds away at arm's length. The camera pulls back as they continue to play and laugh.

Next day they stand aside while a herd of yaks slowly meanders down the trail behind a herdsman. They walk into a gaggle of Tibetan women, who surround them, pushing scarves in their faces for sale.

"Boy," Solveg says, "the only thing more aggressive than a Tibetan trader is his wife!"

A girl, about seven, comes up beside them carrying her baby brother. They're winsome kids, and Eddie falls into conversation. Solveg, who's getting the hang of the language, joins in with some words. Their names are Mingma (Tuesday) and Phongpha.

Solveg takes out a pocket mirror and holds it up to them. They stare and laugh as they begin to understand, then giggle and point to each other.

Eddie takes a look and recoils. He has never seen his beard before and is surprised at how thin his face has grown.

When it's time to shoulder packs again, the kids fall in step, and the four figures trudge up the trail together toward the towering, beckoning, but menacing mountain. At a "Y" in the trail, the kids, now sporting balloon hats, turn off and wave farewell until the Americans disappear around a bend.

"Cute kids," Eddie says.

"Yes," Solveg nods. "And an ecological disaster in the making."

"What do you mean?"

"Look around. Their parents have denuded their mountainsides. There's nothing to hold the rain and snow melt. That means huge floods in Bangladesh next spring, maybe thousands of people killed."

"Yeah, but what else can they do?"

"Bio-gas. There are ways to turn yak dung and garbage into fuel. The Peace Corps can show them how."

Next day Solveg walks ahead, leaving Eddie finishing a sketch. As he resumes his hike, he hears her scream from around a bend ahead: "Eddie! Come quick!"

He runs to her clumsily under his pack.

Solveg is jumping up and down excitedly. "Look!" she cries. "We can have a *bath!*" She pulls him off the trail to a hot spring bubbling in a pool beside a rock. Solveg throws her jacket off and pulls her sweater over her head.

"You go ahead," Eddie says, moving off. "I'll wait."

"Nonsense," Solveg says. "We don't have time to waste. You use that end, and I'll use this." They turn their backs to each other and undress. Solveg unties her pigtails and gives her head a shake until the hair cascades over her shoulders.

While two Nepalese urchins peek and giggle from behind a rock, Solveg and Eddie submerge up to their necks with blissful smiles, turn to each other, and kick the water with their feet. She splashes him, and he does the same as they both laugh.

"Have you got a razor?" she asks. Eddie, naked, climbs out and hastens to get one from his pack and tosses it to her.

Then Solveg, equally naked, climbs out and squats beside her pack, pulling out her dirty laundry, and steps back into the water. He follows her example, and they begin scrubbing, pounding, and rinsing.

A pair of shorts gets away from him and floats into the main channel toward the river. "Well," says Eddie, "I guess he's going to rejoin all the other lost underpants in the great world underwear soul." With a laugh Solveg impulsively picks up a bra and tosses it behind the shorts.

She motions Eddie to turn around, and she goes over his back with a soapy cloth, turns him, and repeats it on his chest. Then she presents her back, sweeps her hair up in back with one hand, inclines her neck, and passes him the soap over her shoulder. Eddie lathers his hand, inhaling the scent of her hair, and slowly soaps her neck, her shoulders, one arm, the other. He follows the contour under her raised arm to her breast.

She closes her eyes and relaxes against him. Slowly she turns toward him, and they gently kiss. He takes her chin in his hand and lifts her face to his, and kisses her again. Suddenly she cups a hand behind his neck and kisses him aggressively.

The camera watches pants and a bra bob and swirl in the current until they are sucked under the rushing waters and disappear together.

The camera slowly lifts toward the mountain, passes the snow line, and continues upward to the peaks and the clouds. We hear laughter as "Solveg's Song" swells and the camera pans across the peaks.

Back on the road, Solveg and Eddie walk along with socks, shorts, panties, and bras drying on their packs and dangling from hiking sticks over their shoulders.

"Where did you learn... that?" Eddie asks.

"What?" (She pretends not to understand.)

"You know...."

"Oh," She tosses her head coquettishly and mimics him: "I haven't just been laying around drinking martinis. I've picked up a few things, too, you know."

Then her knees buckle.

"Whew," she says sitting down to catch her breath. "I guess. . . I'm. . . out of shape. . . . I'm not used to. . . . you."

She throws herself onto her back, half laughing and half gasping as he falls to his knees beside her, laughing with her. He rolls a joint and lights it, rolls onto his back, and takes a drag. Then he flips it away, and his hand gropes for hers. They watch the clouds scud across the sky and the distant peaks.

Later a light cover of snow dusts the hillsides, and the going is slower as they ascend above the tree line into thinner air.

"Man, I've got a splitting headache," Eddie moans.

"Oh-oh," Solveg says. "Altitude sickness. You've got to drink more. It's the best way to cure it."

"But I've already had two quarts today," Eddie protests.

"You need four a day," she commands, "if you want to get over the pass."

"Four! I'm already going to the *chuppi* [latrine] three times every night."

"I don't care," she says. "If you don't go five times a night, you're not drinking enough." He makes a face and takes another gulp from his thermos. "And don't feel bad about the headaches," she says. "After he climbed Mount Everest, Sir Edmund Hillary got altitude sickness so bad he could never go above fourteen thousand feet again. We're at sixteen thousand now, so you're doing better than Sir Edmund."

A simple rock cairn sits beside the trail. Towering above it is Annapurna, a snow plume blowing from the top. Into a rock at the base of the cairn are carved eight names of climbers who have died on the mountain. The last two names are Allison Chadwick and Vera Watson.

"We don't know how they died," Solveg says. "The Sherpas refused to go with them. They were roped together, and one must have slipped and pulled the other with her. They never recovered the bodies." She fights her emotions as she gently brushes dirt from the names.

Several Tibetan travelers pause to watch as she motions to Eddie, who goes into his pack and brings out two white scarves and hands one to Solveg. She lifts one of the rocks and places a scarf under it. He does the same with the second scarf.

They stand silently, then

Solveg begins to sing very softly an old Quaker hymn. Eddie picks it up and softly joins her:

"'Tis a gift to be simple,

'Tis a gift to be free.

'Tis a gift to come down

To where we want to be."

They pause, not knowing what else to say. "I think they died happy," Solveg murmurs. "They were doing what they wanted to do."

"And," Eddie mumbles, "they helped two other women make it, so they really did conquer the mountain."

Solveg shakes her head. "No one 'conquers' a mountain. We stand on the summit for a few minutes, then the wind blows our footsteps away."

They look silently upward to the peak.

"See that narrow spine?" She points. "They were just coming off that when they were blown off. There was life on one side, death on the other, and only a few inches between the two. . . ."

"How precious life is, Eddie." Solveg takes his hand. "How much we should treasure it. Live each day to the fullest. That's the best memorial."

Finally Solveg signs "*Namaste*." Eddie crosses himself, then also signs "*Namaste*." The Tibetans silently join them.

Then she turns and heads down the trail, the strains of the hymn echoing in the mountain air.

At dusk they arrive at a pueblo city of rocks and its hotel. "Maurice Herzog stopped here in 1950 when he climbed Annapurna," she says.

She orders 16 glasses of cold boiled water. "You better drink at least a gallon," she says. "That's eight glasses."

He grimaces and takes a long swallow - "*unk, unk, unk.*"

"More!" she orders. Still making a face, he finishes the glass and puts it upside down on the table. She pushes another in front of him.

"What about you?"

She downs a glass in two draughts, smiles, and nods to him. Grumpily, he drinks and turns that glass up empty.

About 20 minutes later, with 16 upturned glasses on the table, they bolt for the door and the *chuppi* out back. He wins the race, and gallantly stands aside for her, then waits in agony, shifting weight from foot to foot. Finally he hops around behind the *chuppi*, emerging with a happy look of relief on his face.

Under the covers in the moonlight, Solveg asks if Eddie has ever read Maurice Herzog's book, *Annapurna*. He shakes his head. "The people were very hospitable. They brought out young girls for his entire party. Maurice shook his head politely, so the town elders nodded and brought out young boys instead." She laughs.

That night snow is falling and the wind picks up as four porters with heavy burdens make their way in front of their lodge. The men are wearing short pants and are shod only in *zori* slippers. Eddie watches them winding their way up the trail. Soon a bonfire flickers on the mountainside in the night.

Eddie go searches through his duffel. He pulls out two extra sets of thermal underwear and tucks them under his arm and goes out into the dark, bent into the wind, heading toward the fire. He hears footsteps behind him and turns to see a flashlight on the trail. He waits for Solveg to catch up, with her own bundle - a sweater, some T-shirts, and a pair of sneakers.

As they walk into the firelight, the men look up. No emotion registers on their faces. Eddie and Solveg are not sure what to say. What if they're bandits? He thrusts the bundle at the nearest man. She holds out the sweater and sneakers. The men take them wordlessly. Still not knowing what to do, Solveg and Eddie stumble back down the hill.

they lie in their bunks, illuminated by moonlight through the window. Eddie steals out of bed and tiptoes to the door, which creaks although he opens it ever so carefully. A moment later, he tiptoes back, closing the door with another unavoidable creak, and gets back under the covers.

In a minute, Solveg tiptoes to the door, eases it open, and slips out. She comes back just as cautiously with another faintly audible creak.

From outside the hostel, we hear the constant noise of the creaking door opening and closing as two figures in the moonlight duck into the *chuppi* or the bushes and back.

They get up before dawn to begin the final climb to the pass. The stillness is suddenly broken. Sonofabitch!" Eddie curses.

"What's the matter?"

"Look at my pack! My kaopectate bottle froze and burst all over everything!" He shows her a gooey pink mess. She tries not to laugh but can't help herself. At last he can't hold it back either, and the laughter bubbles out.

The pass lies ahead. "We should reach it by noon," Solveg says, pulling a ski mask over her face. "Did you bring one of these?"

"No, why?"

"You've got to wear something over your nose and mouth to hold the moisture in and prevent altitude sickness." Eddie fishes in his pack and brings out some dirty socks.

"They'll have to do," she says. Solveg knots three of them together and wraps them around his face and neck like a scarf, while Eddie emits muffled gagging sounds. Thus bundled, he promptly stumbles in the snow.

"Are you okay?"

"Hell, no! Now my sun glasses are all steamed up - I can't see anything."

"Hold onto my belt, then," Solveg says, leading the way. Breathing is hard. "We have to go slow. Take two breaths on each step instead of one."

As they trudge higher in slow motion, the snow grows deeper beside the trail. As the sun comes out, the day warms up. She nervously eyes the snow above them, glistening as the sun warms it. They stop to rest. "I gotta go," Solveg says.

"Me too."

"You go that way, and I'll go this."

Eddie clumps slowly off. Removing his parka is laborious. First he has to take off his gloves, which he does very slowly in the rarefied air. Then he slowly unbuckles his belt and gradually drops his pants.

Finished, he slowly pulls his pants back up in excruciatingly slow pantomime, re-buckles his belt, and, one arm at a time, puts his pack back on. Then he must put the mittens on. The first one takes ages. The second one is even harder, because he can't use his mittened hand to help get his bare hand in. After many grunts and failures, he finally gets it on and with stiff legs crunches back through the snow to rejoin Solveg. They resume their ponderous march toward the pass.

Suddenly the wind has stopped. A deafening quiet envelopes them. For a few seconds they look at each other, puzzled. Suddenly Solveg understands.

"Run!"

They drop their packs and crunch as fast as they can through the knee-deep snow, pursued by a boiling white wave. The altitude and snow turn their flight into slow motion while the white mass bears down on them, closer and closer.

Eddie grabs Solveg's hand and pulls, but they are thrown head over heels, like surfers wiping out.

Everything turns black.

The trail is white and silent again. A foot is seen sticking out of the snow. Then a hand breaks though. Eddie emerges, dazed, and shakes the snow off. He grabs his left arm and winces in pain.

Wildly he looks around for Solveg. Nothing. He cups his hands and calls her name. No reply. He hears the mountain creaking like a great ship in a storm and realizes that his shout could touch off another avalanche. He wallows through the new snow, desperately looking in every direction.

"Eddie...." He hears a small voice. He whirls around, looking, looking. "Eddie...." He follows the sound. Solveg lies half-buried, and he thrashes toward her.

With his one good arm, Eddie uncovers one leg, then the other. Furiously he digs the snow away from her face. "Don't touch the leg," she winces weakly. "It hurts."

Looking about, Eddie finds one pack jutting half out of the snow and heads for it. He drags it painfully back to Solveg, who is shivering violently He succeeds in opening the pack with one hand, finds a chocolate bar, and gives it to her. She bites hungrily, getting chocolate all over her face.

He hunts through the pack for the thermos bottle. The tea is still warm, and he lifts her head to drink it. Working slowly, Eddie pulls the bedroll out of the pack. He tries to dig a cave in the snow, but it is hard with only one arm. She pulls herself on her arms over to him, and they both dig. At last they have a shelter.

Eddie manages to unzip the bag and slowly pulls it up around Solveg's legs as she bites her lips in pain. He finally gets it snuggly around her shoulders, then he crawls in beside her and slowly zips the bag up around them. He puts his good arm under her head and one leg over hers.

Solveg is shaking, and her teeth chatter. She is trying to say something: "Lau... Laur..." Eddie leans close to listen. At last he catches a word: "Laurie." She repeats it: "Laurie.... I saw Laurie...."

Then:

"K-k-k-*ki*.... G-great *ki*... Y-y-you have great *ki* too." She holds his shoulder tight, and they lie together, huddling to warm each other.

At daylight they are wakened by voices speaking Nepali. The four porters peer at them with concern and hold out tea and rice.

Slowly Solveg and Eddie crawl out of their bag. The men confer.

They take off their coats, revealing their new thermals and their "A Woman"s Place" T-shirts. They tie the coats together for a sled for Solveg.

She smiles but refuses. She's feeling stronger. "I want to walk the whole way," she says.

The porters understand. One of them takes the pack and easily swings it onto one shoulder, then adds his own pack to the other shoulder. Strong and wiry, he seems lost beneath his twin load. Solveg and Eddie weakly protest, but he bobs his head to them and starts off up the trail. Hobbling with one arm on Eddie's good shoulder, Solveg painfully follows, surrounded by the hovering porters.

Once on top, they gaze at a thrilling sight. On the other side Dauligiri Peak raises its mighty head. Far below it, they can just make out the silver thread of the Kola Gandakhi river. The porters smile and point ahead, and Solveg lifts her binoculars.

"There it is!" she shouts, handing the glasses to Eddie and pointing.

He peers, focuses, and finally sees it - a monastery on the side of the mountain. "It's Pisang!" she cries joyfully and hugs him as Beethoven's "Ode to Joy" fills the air. With new energy, they start down.

They limp into the monastery, where the monks welcome them with great concern. The abbott comes in, smiling, and Solveg and

Eddie kneel before him, bowing and murmuring, "*Namaste.*" He also kneels and extends two white scarves to them. They offer theirs in return. They join the monks in a silent meal and listen to their prayers.

At night Solveg and Eddie snuggle together, reading their favorite book by flashlight.

Eddie: "A wager should be laid as to which will get hold of the lips of the other first. If the woman loses, she should pretend to cry, should keep her lover off by shaking her hands and turn away from him and dispute him, saying, 'Let another wager be laid.'"

The flashlight rolls away, leaving the lovers in the dark as we hear the playful yips of their battle, Solveg retrieves the flashlight and resumes reading:

"When a man bites a woman forcibly, she should angrily do the same to him with double force" - she tries, but he pushes her laughingly away - "and she should at once begin a love quarrel with him. She should take hold of her lover by the hair and bend his head down and kiss his lower lip, and then, being intoxicated with love, she should shut her eyes and bite him in various places."

She grabs Eddie's hair and pulls him down.

A new day. Solveg and Eddie walk hand-in-hand. "Look!" she cries bending down to pick up a black stone. "I think it's a fossil!" As they inspect it, it slips out of her hand and shatters, revealing a shrimp-like crustacean form inside. "What's a shrimp doing in the Himalayan mountains?"

"Well, this all was under water millions of years ago," Eddie says, "before India slammed into China and pushed the mountains up out of the sea."

"Look, the two halves fit together perfectly." She lowers her eyes. "Like us." She gives Eddie one half, and she keeps the other. They kiss.

Back at the monastery they sit together, holding hands and gazing at the mountains. "Did you find Laurie?" Eddie asks softly.

Solveg slowly nods. "Oh yes. I saw her as clearly as I'm seeing you right now. She made me call out to you."

"And what about yourself? Have you found her?"

Solveg shrugs. "A little of her. I'll probably be looking for me for the rest of my life…. What about you? Have you found Eddie?"

He shakes his head. "No. I lost him. I don't think he'll ever come back."

They sit silently.

"What about God?" Eddie asks. "Did you find Him?"

Solveg thinks a minute and takes a deep breath. "I don't know, Eddie. I'm still not sure if there is a God." They watch silently as the setting sun casts a pink *alpen* glow on Annapurna and the temple gong resounds across the valley. "But if there is a God, He must be here."

That night, sharing a cell in the monastery, they embrace in the nude by the light of a flickering yak-butter lamp. He reaches for the camera, but she stops him with a hand.

"Please," he says.

"Pictures fade," she whispers with a kiss. "Photograph me with your eyes - that will last as long as we do." She steps back, shakes her hair free, and strikes a pose.

It is midnight. "Solveg's Song." Eddie is asleep on his back. Solveg rests on one elbow, watching him. Slowly she leans toward him. She says softly, almost as if praying, "When a woman looks at the face of her lover while he is asleep and kisses it to show her desire, it is called 'the kiss that kindles love.'" She slowly bends down to him, her hair falling across her cheek, drawing a veil over them both.

Morning. They are in their sleeping bags, hands intertwined. She rests her head against his and rubs her cheek against his beard, which has grown since the trek began.

He smiles, kisses her hair, and embraces her, She embraces him back. "I've never met anyone like you, Solveg," he says. "I don't want to lose you."

Solveg fights emotion. "Oh, Eddie, we can't."

"What do you mean?"

"You should have kids. I can't start a family again at my age."

"We'll work it out," he says desperately. "You know what 'The Book' says: "If men and women act according to each other's liking, their love for each other will not be lessened even in a hundred years."

Her chin quivers as she tries to smile.

"Is it another man?"

"Oh, darling, there *is* no other man like you." He rests his head on her breast, and she kisses his hair.

"Then...?"

"Eddie, you remember *Lost Horizons?*"

"Yeah. Everyone is happy, and people live to be two hundred years old, and they still look like they're twenty, and Ronald Colman falls in love with a beautiful girl."

"Remember, the *lama* warns him that she must never leave her home in the valley. But he takes her away with him anyway, across Shangri La pass through a blizzard, leaving her lovely valley behind. And as they struggle through the snow, he looks at her, and she has become a wrinkled, old woman faltering in the storm."

Eddie tries to speak, but she stops him.

"Dearest, I don't want that to happen to us. You've made me feel young and beautiful again. The only way I can stay young and beautiful forever is in your heart. Twenty years from now you'll be thirty-eight, and I'll be sixty-one. I want us to be in love with each other then just as we are now. You and I have found something that almost no other two people in history have had. Oh, Eddie, darling, remember me like this always."

Solveg lifts Eddie's head from her breast, lies back and wraps her arms around his neck, and slowly pulls him down onto her.

The next day a brilliant sun bathes the mountain peak. It is a holy day, and Solveg and Eddie watch the monks take down last year's withered evergreen decorations and tattered prayer flags and put up new ones. A boy monk hands the guests a piece of white cloth and a brush and smilingly indicates they should write something.

Solveg dips the brush in the ink, thinks for a minute, and draws a single palm. She hands the brush to Eddie, who draws a second palm joining hers. They hand the cloth back to the boy, who attaches it to the rope with other prayers. Several monks raise the line and string it securely between two walls. Solveg and Eddie watch the flags snap in the brisk wind.

At the Kathmandu airport, "On Top of Old Smoky" softly plays as Solveg and Eddie each place a white scarf around the other's neck, then stand diffidently, waiting for the flight to be called. She leans lightly on a cane. His beard has been trimmed short and neat. He stands lean and tall.

"No more baby fat," she teases, with a mock pat on the tummy.

"Yeah," he tries to joke. "I can see my toes again." They force smiles.

"What will you do, Eddie?"

"I'm not sure. The Peace Corps is building a plant back up the trail to make apple cider. I think I'll go back and help on that for a while. After that, probably art school."

"What will your father say?"

"He'll just have to get used to it, I guess. And you?"

"Go to Idaho and teach school on a reservation. You know me and kids and mountains."

Solveg unzips her belt pouch and brings out some color prints. "Remember these?" He sorts through them, smiling at the shots of him making balloon hats, playing frisbee, slumping with fatigue, carrying his laundry on his stick etc etc. He starts to return them, but she pushes them back.

He unrolls several pages of his sketches - Rod and Dolly, Itchy and Keiko, the kids, the lodges, the porters, Pisang, the abbott. And many pages of her. She smiles at each one. "They're wonderful, Eddie." her voice breaks a little.

"They're for you".

"This is my favorite." She shows him a page of her splashing him at the hot spring and doing her laundry, looking up at him with a surprised smile on her face. She gives it back with a demure half-smile: "You keep this one, dear."

The flight is announced. They look at each other desperately. They embrace, murmuring. Their lips brush.

She breaks it off. "Remember," she whispers. "In Nepali there is no word for thank you or love."

The notes of Óld Smoky" fade, replaced by "Ritsum Tiri Die," played slowly and sadly.

"God be with you," he says.

"He is. And with you."

They squeeze hands. Solveg turns and walks to the plane. At the door she looks back, her hands gesturing *namaste* and her lips forming "God be with you."

His hands and lips reply.

Then she is gone. "Solveg's Song" sneaks in on the sound track and gradually grows stronger. Eddie slips his hand into his pocket and brings out the fossil, which he rubs as the plane takes off and climbs against a snow-capped mountain.

At Pisang monks chant, a plane crosses the sky, prayer flags whip in the wind, and "Solveg's Song" wells up.

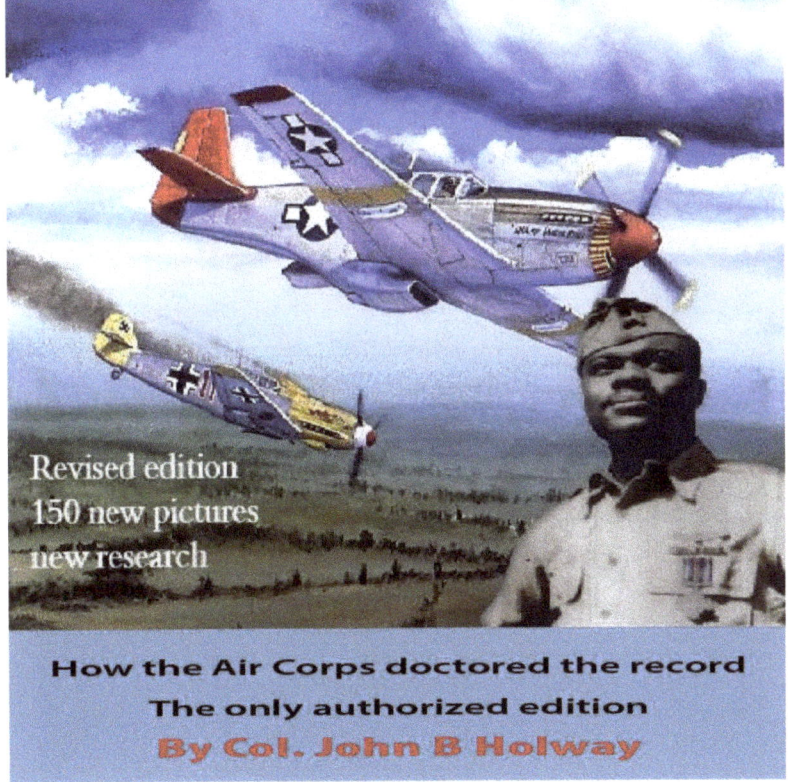

A major motion
picture by George Lucas

An important and inspirational work. Holway wisely allows the veterans ample room to tell their tales in their own words, and they provide keen insights into both social and aviation history.
Publishers' Weekly

Holway's work as a collective biography is an important addition to any African-American history and/or military studies collection.
Library Journal

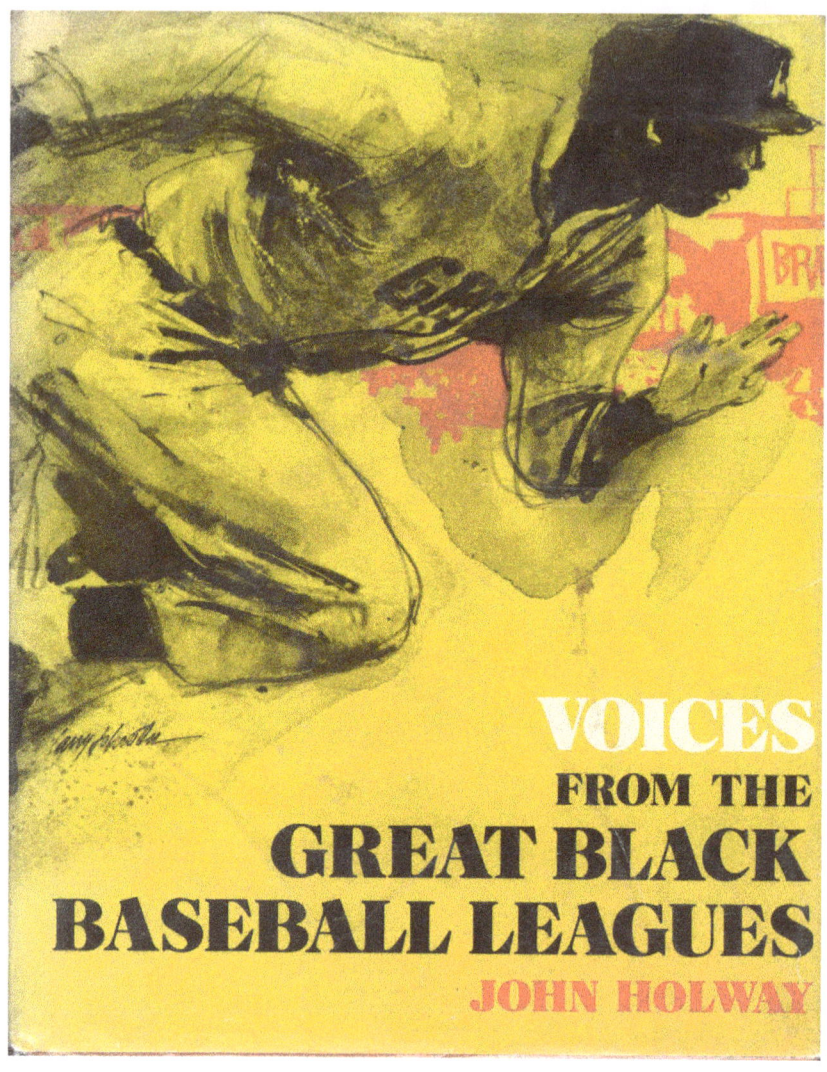

Holway has edited length interviews into richly detailed story-telling gems, The games are re-played in the reader's mind. It is the closest we can come to seeing them. These men would have been super-stars as surely as Babe Ruth and the rest. **The New York Times.**

This book busts over the fence revealing personality as few sports books do. **Washington Star.**

Winner, Casey award, best baseball book of 1988

Holway's statistics prove the greatness of the Negro League players. Now we can truly call baseball the National Pasttime. **Ken Burns**

Holway, one of the deans of black baseball history, provides the most complete statistical study yet of the game's segregated half. **Library Journal**

Compelling. A must-read for all baseball fans. **Allan 'Bud' Selig, Commissioner of baseball**.

Holway writes in lively fashion. The research is impressive. A striking overview. **The Book Reader**

A wonderful collection of profiles. **The Washington Post**

An important historical corrective. **Publishers Weekly**

The most up-to-date compendium on the game's most important position… It's a bag of peanuts - reach in and take as much as you like. The years of research have produced a mound of gourmet goobers…. daunting knowledge and contagious affection for baseball. **Sports Illustrated.**

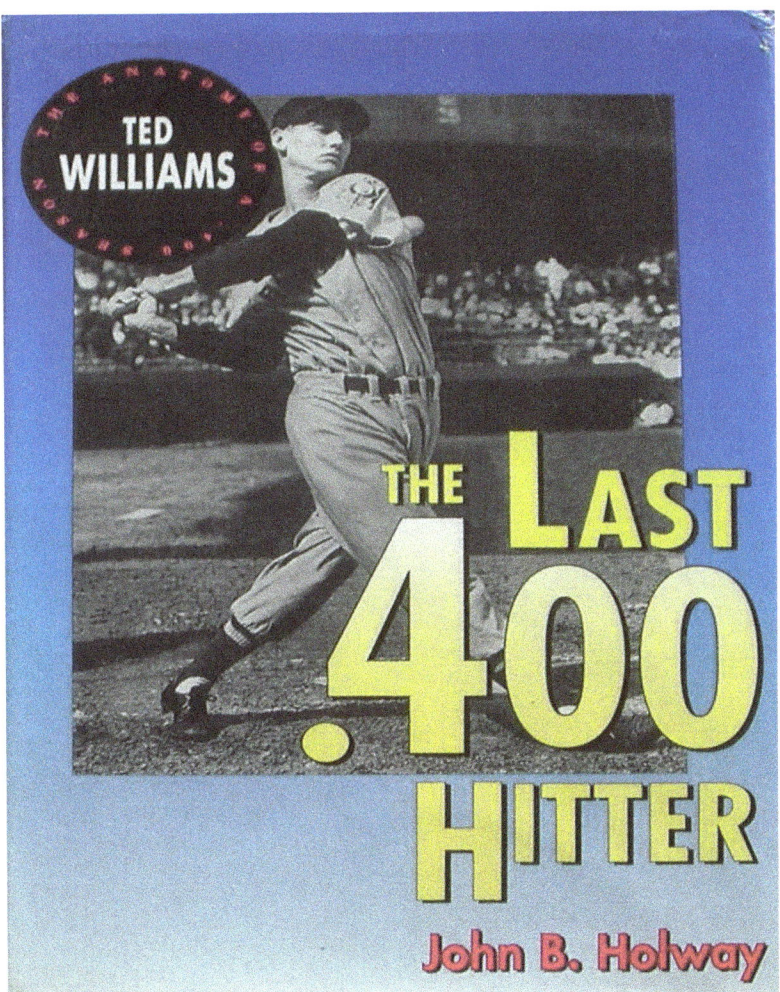

Great fun. Holway has skillfully revived a remarkable period in baseball history, as well as the turbulent world surrounding it. I thoroughly enjoyed reliving those times through this insightful book. **Jean Yawkey, owner, Boston Red Sox.**

What a delight! Superbly researched and vividly written. A sure winner. **Merritt Abrash, Professor, Renssalear Polytechnic Institute**

Holway's statistics prove the greatness of the Negro League players. Now we can truly call baseball the National Pasttime. **Ken Burns**

I also have a three-hour TV series ready for camera:

**They called Mule Samson the black Babe Ruth.
Others called Ruth the white Mule Samson**

Kick Mule

"You were the pioneers. You made it possible for us."

Willie Mays

www.ingramcontent.com/pod-product-compliance
Lightning Source LLC
Chambersburg PA
CBHW041312110526
44591CB00022B/2890